Natural Grace

God and Nature in our Slice of Pennsylvania

Thomas Ask

For the glory of God.

ISBN-13: 978-1974589647

ISBN-10: 1974589641

Cover Photograph: McIntyre Wild Area, Rock Run, Ralston, PA by Thomas Ask

Scripture quotations are from the ESV® Bible (The Holy Bible, English Standard Version®), copyright © 2001 by Crossway, a publishing ministry of Good News Publishers. Used by permission. All rights reserved.

Printed in the United States of America

Contents

For you shall go out in joy and be led forth in peace; the mountains and the hills before you shall break forth into singing, and all the trees of the field shall clap their hands. (Isaiah 55:12)

Foreword

I'm not from this area. I'm originally from Illinois. I moved to northern Pennsylvania a couple of decades ago and became impressed by the natural beauty. We have woods, rivers, meadows, and mountains. We have all four seasons. We can do all sorts of outdoor activities. This part of the state has endless green mountains and streaming rivers. The area has largely recovered from the extractive industries of timber and coal that changed its appearance. But the mountains and rivers didn't change; they shrugged off these industries and the forests and meadows recovered (usually). There are some orange rocks and stands of larch trees that point to the environmental challenges of the past, but they remind us of the tough part of our natural history.

We measure the seasons by the sights, sounds, and smells of nature. The spring season calls out from the rising spikes of skunk cabbage and hosta plants to the wafting of blossoming trees. It is fun to break off a bit of the skunk cabbage while still wearing winter clothes and savor the pungent odor of new growth. We then move from the heat and dark green of summer into the brilliance and crispness of autumn. Finally, winter arrives and everything seems to rest and wait while we drink hot cocoa and snuggle into our homes.

This book is not an adoration of nature.[1] It is not about how God is in nature but rather how God is shown by nature. Nature must never be idolized. As Charles Spurgeon noted, "Idolatry is the greatest insult the creature can offer the Creator." As we engage nature, we unpack deeper levels of truth about ourselves and our relationship with God. We are the pinnacle of God's creation – image bearers of God. "I am fearfully and wonderfully made," said David in Psalm 139. God gave us stewardship of His creation, but the nature we enjoy also declares His glory.

I have always loved nature, from tunneling into snow banks to making tree forts to taking long walks. The cliffs and lakes, bogs and hills, caves and trees are all playgrounds with ready-made toys. I think everyone loves being in nature. It is a primal need that satisfies us with images and sounds we can't articulate.

This book ended up being more autobiographical than I intended. Perhaps that underscores the relational aspect of faith. Our desire for relationships with others shadows God's desire to have a relationship with us.

This is an introduction to my simple life in God's creation and reflections on my inquiries into questions such as the following. *Why is there evil and misery? How do I know I'm saved? How should I pray? How do I discern God's will?* I am not a pastor or theologian and there are many excellent resources that delve into these topics better than I am capable. However, I hope you find these disparate musings helpful as you try to make sense of the world around you.

Part I

"*A man sees in the world what he carries in his heart.*"

Johann Wolfgang von Goethe

Natural Grace

1

Introduction

"It's all yours."

With that, my son Eric tied into the rappel line and stepped carefully off the edge of the cliff. I sat at a nearby outcropping looking out at the far ridge, my peripheral vision in full throttle. Eric eased himself down beyond view and past that microsecond of worry when you are not really sure about the security of your rope. He made his way to the bottom of the cliff and untied. We had finished this part of his "blessing on the cliff" weekend and were now on to the next adventure. Before his solo rappel, we had gone down together on separate ropes and met half way down. There we paused and I spoke words of love and Christ. We enjoyed a tender moment hanging in the vertical world with a rushing stream below us and the whole of nature wrapped around us. I gave him a knife I made from a worm-eaten tropical hardwood and a lot of sandpaper. He was a man in my eyes and I recognized this just like the animals in the woods know when their babies grow up.

Just a few years prior, we were walking out from a short backpacking trip and I did not want it to end. We had talked nonstop the whole time, crammed our bivouac tent into clearings among the mountain laurel and slept with the waiting world outside our rip stop nylon. That trip ended and the child grew. God's grace let me have these times and I was very appreciative.

Grabbing each day is important. They are gifts from God. The value of a day and the importance of our attitude toward a day is appreciated in the secular world also. Dr. Seuss would guide you in your day as follows:

> Congratulations!
> Today is your day!
> You're off to Great Places!
> You're off and away!
>
> You have brains in your head.
> You have feet in your shoes.
> You can steer yourself
> any direction you choose.[1]

My faith in Jesus has given me a peace that passes all understanding. It provides an indescribable joy. The apostle Paul wrote, "What you have learned and received and heard and seen in me – practice these things, and the God of peace will be with you" (Philippians 4:9). While my faith shows many of my imperfections, I am too slow witted to catch most of them. So I wander about offending people, while thinking and doing the wrong things. But God is gracious and merciful. He forgives me for mistakes I don't even recognize. But He blesses me with so much right in my backyard. Together, let's explore the natural wonders of our area while we think of grander things.

* * *

The Dutch philosopher Baruch Spinoza was wrong in saying that God was in nature and when nature is understood so too is God. God is outside the wash of green and browns. He shines through the Holy Spirit, not rustling leaves.

My experiences with God among the natural beauty of our area seem to depend on how I'm feeling and whom I'm with. Being alone also has its marvels. Just listening to the world around me as it intermingles with daydreams and worries gives rise to dreams of great journeys and oceans of experiences. These feelings can't be replicated when I am with others. Being alone and quiet allows for deep thinking. When the distractions are stripped away and I am alone with my own fears and ambitions, I tend to create the grandest aspirations and find the deepest refuges in faith.

Generally, I like to be with people for most of my activities, especially backpacking. However, I do not mind rappelling and downhill skiing by myself. I don't have to rush or worry, I can pause when I like and just find peace. However, riding a ski chair lift up with my kids has brought out joyous conversations, and having my kids belay me when rock climbing has put an exclamation point behind my trust.

The last decades have been fathering years and I have been blessed to have many outdoor adventures with my two children, Eric and Elayna. Introducing them to new experiences and seeing the world through their eyes has added a magical texture to my outdoor experiences. However, my experiences with my wife, Beth, which have more often been in the areas of foreign travel, food and peaceful walks, have more deeply grounded the love we have for Christ and each other.

Enjoying nature is in beautiful agreement with the 10th commandment. Here we are commanded not to covet our neighbors' things. While this commandment speaks to desiring what others have, it can be more fully recognized to assert we should be content with what we have. Our natural beauty is available to everyone. We can all share the sunset and our beautiful creeks. Our forests are widely available for walking and for our wildlife, from birds to bears, to wander across all our yards. There is rich contentment in enjoying nature.

However, we have to be on guard for a false contentment, one of our own making where psychological forces and bird calls can blend into a weirdness not of God's calling but rather from our desire to remove the dissonance that burdens our souls.

The context for adventure is important. The apostle Paul traveled all over the place, but his adventures in the Middle East and Europe were to present the love of Jesus, not to sightsee. The apostle Peter was not being a daredevil when he stepped off a boat and onto the water to meet Jesus – Peter was demonstrating faith. Faith as the context for adventure resounds in the Bible, from Abraham leaving his hometown to explore the western lands to the Israelites wandering in the Sinai desert. We can honor Christ when we engage nature and test our own physical and mental abilities in His creation. We can honor Him by marveling at what He has given us and what He allows us to see and do.

While this whole work is intended as a love letter to Jesus and not a vainglorious autobiography, the role of kids in outdoor activities is hard for me to separate.[2] These outdoor activities become delightfully applied actions, moving from exploring our own abilities to teaching of those things which you love. Teaching adds sweetness to these activities.

2

Backpacking

"How do radios work dad?" Eric asked as we bore our heavy packs up another rise on the West Rim Trail. I drew upon my ham radio background and explained oscillators, amplifiers and antennas. All I really wanted to do was watch my feet go up the trail. I wanted to keep my mind in that groove that contends with discomfort by putting the legs on autopilot. But no, there were questions to be answered by a strong, curious mind. After these backpacking trips when I wanted to enjoy the comfortable car seats and high velocity travel with no worries except the fuel gauge and speedometer, Eric would ask me to tell him a story, as I would do in the tent at bedtime. Recognizing that story-telling was better than zoning out, I would create stories about magical trees and underground kingdoms.

Backpacking is the hardest thing you can do in our area. You haul all the stuff you need on your back and you step out from civilization (including your car!). You are alone with things that want to sting you or lurk around your campsite. All the while, you are sweaty and sore.

In addition, there are not a lot of dramatic things to say about backpacking. You walk a lot, you see a lot of vegetation, you worry about water sources, and you hear strange things at night. When you are done, you are tired and dirty.

However, backpacking puts you deeply into nature. It makes you vulnerable, dirty, and appreciative. You are truly independent. You can travel for one day or for one month with what is on your back. You see and hear things you wouldn't otherwise in the rush of life. Few things make you feel as accomplished as completing your backpacking goal. Not only do you get to live your childhood desire to wear the same clothes all the time and be comfortable with deeply embedded grime, you also appreciate the comforts of home – especially the first shower, good meal, and soft bed.

Backpacking is more of a mental battle than physical one. While contending with soreness and fatigue, you only have a vague sense for the purpose of your journey. However, backpacking provides a great intimacy with nature, a deep separation from civilization and, for me, the most satisfying of all endeavors in the woods. It lets the animal in me breathe.

We have great places to backpack in our area. All the roads running through our woods make it easy to customize your trip to fall within your time schedule. The trails are similar in appearance: hardwood forests and rocks. Not much water and lots of bugs in the springtime. Backpacking lets you break all the rules: you walk where you want, you sleep where you want, and you go to the bathroom where you want. You lie down wherever it pleases you and push yourself to your heart's content. You do worry about things though. Where will be the next source of water? Will I be bitten by ticks and other bugs? Will I find a flat place to set up my tent?

The experiences can be very random, from stepping in bear poop at the very end of a trip to rocks exploding in a campfire. One time we had to tie the car to a tree when we drove out too far up an access road in March that suddenly turned into a sheet of ice and my car started to slide off the road. We gradually lowered it off the ice sheet using rock wedges and rope.

Backpacking can bring some scares. My most frightening experience was somewhat funny. I got up in the middle of the night and unzipped the bivouac tent flap. I was looking outside when someone shone a big flashlight in my face. My heart stopped. Then I realized it was just the full Moon and I had moved my head just enough that it appeared to pop out from behind a tree. Kind of silly, but I remember the scare very well.

The most appealing aspect of backpacking is the utter independence as well as the communion with my kids and nature. Nine hundred years ago, St. Bernard, founder and abbot of Clairvaux, lived as a monk and noted, "You will find something more in woods than in books. Trees and stones will teach you that which you can never learn from masters."

I am humbled by the feeling of descending nightfall – how it makes your world go from grand vistas to a tiny sphere of vision. Darkness changes everything. What was once easy is now difficult. Your most powerful sense, vision, becomes subordinated to hearing. And you hear all sorts of things. I don't like darkness – I like daylight. The joy of daylight while backpacking highlights the metaphor of God being light in 1 John 1:5, "God is light, and in him is no darkness at all."

What a great thought! Fear is pushed back when you can see everything. When bad things, like grunting animals, are not hidden but rather exposed, they run from the exposure. But the sneakiness of darkness is only sneaky when you know you can escape. You can turn on a light or get out of the cave. It is a lot tougher to wait for sunrise.

The sounds of the night also humble you before the Lord of creation. In your home, you control much around you but in the deep woods, you are just a person with some gear. Your tent thankfully keeps out bugs, but the critters know that you are incapacitated by all that nylon and will do all sorts of strange things at night. I always sleep better the second night after I have gotten used to the distinctive noises of the forest, and my self-protection instinct relaxes a bit. Intimacy with nature takes a little more time than what Shakespeare would have opined when he said, "One touch of nature makes the whole world kin." I don't think Shakespeare went backpacking – it takes a couple of days to become kin.

Eric was nine when we did our first backpacking trip. He wanted to carry a big pack. I reluctantly agreed and gave him a full-size pack and loaded it with the lightest and bulkiest things I could think of. He loved it. It was only an overnight trip, hiking in and out on the same path. We had a huge tent and I set it up on a cliff over the creek. I was able to lower a pail down on a rope and get all the water we could want. However, it wasn't the best location. I worried all night about Eric going out of the tent by himself at night and falling off the cliff.

On the way back, he was tired and he tripped several times. I really didn't want him to carry all that weight, but he insisted. The fourth time he tripped, landing on his stomach with a grunting forced exhalation, I said, "Be careful, Eric." I hated saying that. It was a stupid, meaningless statement that only made him feel worse. I just couldn't help myself because his falling frustrated me.

Sometimes it can be hard for parents not to contribute to their children's troubles. "Thanks Dad, now I know to be careful," Eric probably would have liked to say. But he just got up again and plowed on. I was proud of him, no complaining or snarkiness, just resolve. In the same way that Eric put up with me, so God puts up with so much in our lives. Even though He has lovingly warned and admonished us about our misdeeds in the Bible, I just want to keep the sins that are culturally acceptable and historically moderated. But that is not what Scripture declares. 'If you love Jesus, keep His commandments' is the constant refrain in the Bible. Often I ignore what the Bible says, yet get mad at God when I trip. The cycle of sinning and forgiveness must be sad for God to witness. The cycle of justice and mercy is seemingly overtaxed by His people.

We have mainly backpacked on the West Rim Trail. On one trip, we were only a few hours from reaching the end when I was blessed with a rich appreciation of what I was experiencing: I was hiking with a lightened pack, good conversation, clean air, deeply breathing lungs, good health, and a flat trail. All this with my son, and a sea of love around us. I didn't want it to end, which is unusual for me when backpacking. I told Eric how good a time I was having and asked him to promise he would hike the same trip with me in 20 years. We went many times after that but now he is away from home and I have to wait for that 20-year mark to arrive. I know it will never be the same, but that spark still simmers.

Now I backpack with my daughter, Elayna, and she is a real trooper in the woods. We had wonderful experiences the first time Elayna went backpacking. Eric wasn't jealous of our trip and even snuck in an encouraging note in her backpack. Unlike Eric, Elayna didn't mind me carrying most of the gear. She had a small daypack with some clothes and she swooshed through the trail. The next day, we received a delightful smile from Jesus (which is just what I call it) soon before we got back to our car – we found ripe blueberries and gorged on these treats among the lush green foliage and speckled blue sky made by the old hardwood forest.

We usually take two or three-day trips. That is probably not enough time to really get into the raw mode of nature-living, but it is what time and circumstances allow. The trails in our area are usually two-nighters, but a one-night excursion into the woods is a million times better than a no night excursion in the woods. It still humbles you and grounds you in God's creation. We have enjoyed the vistas and the coziness of the woods, the smell of vegetation, and the remarkable wash of white when the mountain laurels are blooming.

Time settles and your vision improves. Georgia O'Keefe relates this even to friendship, saying, "Nobody sees a flower really; it is so small. We haven't time, and to see takes time – like to have a friend takes time." These qualities of time and attention relate easily to Bible study. We should spend time reading the Bible so that we can learn more about Jesus just as we might read a magazine to learn more about your favorite personality or athlete. I struggle with Bible reading. Sometimes I enjoy delightful peace while reading – and sometimes reading the Bible is exactly what I don't want to do.

We have tried variants of our standard backpacking ways. Eric wanted to do a true bushwhacking style of backpacking where we stayed off trails entirely. This was fun and made us feel even further away from civilization than our typical trail-tied trips.

Elayna wanted to do a one day through-hike of the West Rim Trail. Eric and I had done this normally three-day hike in two days once. We were fairly close to the end on the second day and Eric kept pushing us. I was limping because of a bad toe in a bad boot, but I made a walking stick and didn't take off my boot until we were done for fear of what I would see. We made it to the car sometime around 10 p.m. on the second day and my toe eventually healed.

Elayna wanted to beat this record by going ultralight and doing it in one day. I always end up bringing way too much food on our trips, so deciding what to bring was a fun and enjoyable part of our conversations for weeks prior to the trip. We wanted to come back hungry.

For this trip, Beth and I drove two cars from our home to the West Rim Trail's northern terminus near Wellsboro, and then Beth dropped us off at the southern terminus near Blackwell. By the time we were done with all of this, it was 10 a.m. – kind of late for a no-sleep through-hike. But that is how we started. Fortunately, the weather was perfect, with sunshine and dry air. We carried daypacks with a bit of food, sweaters, headlamps, a water filter, and a large garbage bag. It was incredibly liberating to travel with such a light load. We felt like we were flying as we rapidly made our way through this familiar path. When we got to the Bradley Wales rest area in the early evening, we met a man who was taking a group of young people backpacking. He was very gracious and even applauded us and presented us to his youth group as we passed their campsite. We felt both proud and awkward as we hustled past.

After the sun set, we got out our headlamps and made our way down the trail. We got disoriented a couple of times and even had to make our way around a collapsed bridge in the dark. We rested a few times and then finally, around 1 a.m., we decided to sleep for a while. We took out the plastic garbage bags we brought, tore open the sides, and laid them out in a small clearing. Utterly exhausted, we laid down on them and fell immediately asleep. Then it started to rain. The rain was a cold kiss from heaven and I pulled out my garbage bag from under me and laid it over me. I told Elayna to do the same. I tried to go back to sleep but the garbage bag wasn't keeping me cozy. I checked with Elayna who was lying near me and she was awake too so we decided to get up and go back to hiking. We were groggy and stiff, but we got back on the trail and managed our way through some confusing turns using our map and compass. It was harder to discern where we were when it was dark and we were tired. It was a challenge to think clearly in the drizzle with a paper map, a simple compass, and wet glasses. It was humbling to see how my mind was not working properly.

We finally got to the end of the trail right before sunrise and we were very happy. It was amazing how fun and fast the first part of the trip was and how

21

physically and mentally difficult the second part was. All due to darkness and fatigue.

Being disoriented can come in our life when we don't fully embrace and submit to God's instructions for living, as found in the Bible. When we obey the easy parts of the Bible, it is as if we are carrying our light daypacks. We walk quickly and easily. But when it is dark and you're exhausted the "easy" parts aren't enough. You have to understand God condemns gossip in the same breath as He condemns haters of God; envy in the same breath as murder (Romans 1:29-30). God can't look at sin, and even though we hide behind Jesus' righteousness, we need to obey the difficult parts of the Bible and accept Jesus not only as our Savior, but also as our Lord. It is not in our American tradition to accept a 'lord' of our life. Nevertheless, that is where we must put Jesus.

On the few occasions we have backpacked on Sunday, we would start our day with breakfast and then walk away from the campsite, and I would ask the kids where they wanted to have church. Eric or Elayna would identify a suitable spot, whatever that might mean for them, and we would flop into the warmly decaying and soft layers of leaves for our "church in the woods". There we would sing, read Scripture, and enjoy the richness of intimate prayers with Jesus – short, heartfelt, and awash in declarations of God's glory. On the Lord's Day, we should gather with other believers, but there are times when a church in the woods is as close as we can get.

Misery

Backpacking does not make a very dramatic story. It is a lot of walking with occasional misery becoming the peculiar highlights. Being wet, cold, dirty, hungry, or thirsty can be part of the journey. It doesn't have to be that way at all, but when these miseries arise, they seem to provide the stories we share with others and make the backpacking experience distinct from our normal lives. These exclamation points can really drive an experience deeply into our memory.

One time, I was sleeping outside in the forest near my tiny namesake town north of Oslo, Norway (yes, the town's name is 'Ask'). It was a cold night, and I thought I would just sleep on the ground under the pine trees with my warm sleeping bag keeping me snuggled and cozy. There was a fluttering of snowfall that added some sparkle to the deep, dark forest. However, while I was sleeping, the weather warmed up just enough for the gentle snowfall to turn to a gentle drizzle – a delightfully unobtrusive cold drizzle. By the time the rain woke me up, my down sleeping bag was completely saturated and I was quickly getting cold. I grabbed all my gear and tried to find shelter from the cold drizzle. I found an old shed and sat through the night shivering. A never-forgotten nasty night to remind me of my visit to my grandfather's hometown.

I can understand why Satan tempted Jesus in the wilderness after He was lonely, hungry and tired. At that point, Jesus was digging beyond human reserves. He was feeding from the love of His Father, where the bread of Heaven was a real subsistence for Him. We can also tap into this bread knowing that Jesus suffered under these challenges fully as a man. We are humbled by Jesus, the greatest backpacker.

Jesus encountered all the temptations and trials that we can imagine. And it was for the purpose described in Hebrews 4:14-16:

> Since then we have a great high priest who has passed through the heavens, Jesus, the Son of God, let us hold fast our confession. For we do not have a high priest who is unable to sympathize with our weaknesses, but one who in every respect has been tempted as we are, yet without sin. Let us then with confidence draw near to the throne of grace, that we may receive mercy and find grace to help in time of need.

As sinners, a fallen people, we naturally wish to follow Satan. We are the "sons of disobedience" as described in Ephesians 2:1-3:

And you were dead in the trespasses and sins in which you once walked, following the course of this world, following the prince of the power of the air, the spirit that is now at work in the sons of disobedience – among whom we all once lived in the passions of our flesh, carrying out the desires of the body and the mind, and were by nature children of wrath, like the rest of mankind.

The proclamation continues, telling how God responded to our condition in Ephesians 2:4-9:

But God, being rich in mercy, because of the great love with which he loved us, even when we were dead in our trespasses, made us alive together with Christ – by grace you have been saved — and raised us up with him and seated us with him in the heavenly places in Christ Jesus, so that in the coming ages he might show the immeasurable riches of his grace in kindness toward us in Christ Jesus. For by grace you have been saved through faith. And this is not your own doing; it is the gift of God, not a result of works, so that no one may boast.

The woods can strip us of stability, safety, support and familiarity. We need to recognize Satan's active role in deceiving. This is a key insight needed for Christians to manage their life. Love God and your neighbor while running from Satan. In 1 Peter 5:6-11, the Christian walk is well described:

> Humble yourselves, therefore, under the mighty hand of God so that at the proper time he may exalt you, casting all your anxieties on him, because he cares for you. Be sober-minded; be watchful. Your adversary the devil prowls around like a roaring lion, seeking someone to devour. Resist him, firm in your faith, knowing that the same kinds of suffering are being experienced by your brotherhood throughout the world. And after you have suffered a little while, the God of all grace, who has called you to his eternal glory in Christ, will himself restore, confirm, strengthen, and establish you. To him be the dominion forever and ever. Amen.

We don't consider suffering good, but we do call the results of suffering good. The suffering has some purpose that we might not be able to understand. James 1:2 and Philippians 3:11 remind us to be content under any circumstances. We are content because we know that in the end we will be with God forever and free of evil and misery. Dealing with tough conditions now calls us to remember with a deeper joy that our salvation is preserved in God's hands. And joy is a fruit of the Spirit. The long view, beyond the temporal and the simple provisions of life, are described in 1 Timothy 6:6-10:

But godliness with contentment is great gain, for we brought nothing into the world, and we cannot take anything out of the world. But if we have food and clothing, with these we will be content. But those who desire to be rich fall into temptation, into a snare, into many senseless and harmful desires that plunge people into ruin and destruction.

It is okay to run from a roaring lion – in fact, it is wise. Our ammunition is Scripture. This is why Scripture is called the "sword of the Spirit" in Ephesians. We also have faith as our defense. Ephesians 6:16 tells us we should "take up the shield of faith, with which you can extinguish all the flaming darts of the evil one."

Dealing with suffering in a spiritual way sounds vague and hard to grasp. The spiritual element of suffering can only be approached by faith. And our faith is imperfect. I don't like to suffer and I struggle to find spiritual refuge at these times. But this is my struggle and I keep straining towards the goal of having Jesus' thoughts become my thoughts.

3

Climbing

I went rock climbing when I was a kid and it was scary. We didn't use ropes, just childlike athleticism and sufficient care. I did a little technical climbing in college, but I had no special abilities with it. Many years ago during a family vacation, we stopped in Moab, Utah where Eric and I went rock climbing with a guide. We loved it, and Eric climbed like a goat. When we got back, I bought some minimal gear and looked for places to climb. I practiced my knots and technique using the basement support column, and later our small tree house. I scoured the area for cliffs. The ones closest to our house were crumbly shale. Finally, I found some cliffs near Rock Run and gave them all silly names. There was 'Kids' Cliff,' where I first took Eric and later Elayna. It was only 15 feet high but it was wide and you could explore along the face. It was an easy climb, but it allowed me to play in the vertical world. Over 2,500 years ago, the philosopher Heraclitus noted, "Man is most nearly himself when he achieves the seriousness of a child at play." Even as adults, we enjoy finding a new playground.

Later I found a beautiful, tall cliff. This cliff was not really good for climbing, but it was a lot of fun to rappel down. Rock Run's stream roared near the base and it was easily accessed from the road. We climbed some other cliffs in our area, but these were our favorite cliffs – close to home and offering thrills and intimacy with stone.

I took many friends to these cliffs, many of which could be top roped or just rappelled down. I found it beautiful that $300 worth of equipment in a ripped-up backpack could take me into a different world where my face was inches from beautiful stone and the wind danced and swirled. Plants scratched out a life in small fissures, and the red and white-streaked rocks were warm to the touch. I could stand on a ledge halfway up and just absorb beauty. Jesus would smile and share His creation, His love for my place in this world. I would often be alone on these cliffs and draw so deeply from the air that I felt fully satisfied.

These are the snippets of deep satisfaction I get from nature that point to something greater. In John 6,

Jesus makes clear the spiritual reality of being truly satisfied by referring to the food God provided the Jews during their wilderness exile.

> Our fathers ate the manna in the wilderness; as it is written, 'He gave them bread from heaven to eat.' Jesus then said to them, "Truly, truly, I say to you, it was not Moses who gave you the bread from heaven, but my Father gives you the true bread from heaven. For the bread of God is he who comes down from heaven and gives life to the world." They said to him, "Sir, give us this bread always." Jesus said to them, "I am the bread of life, whoever comes to me shall not hunger, and whoever believes in me shall never thirst." (John 6:31-35)

We get our ultimate satisfaction from Christ.

One day, I was especially blessed. I parked my car on the side of a dirt road and decided to explore – just walk into the woods and up a mountain to see what I could see. I grabbed surfaced tree roots, dug in my boots, and made my way up the steep incline coming from the road. I walked up toward the top of an ill-defined ridge that is common in our area. I hiked up and up, my feet slipping when I did not use the edge of my boot to cut into the loamy soil where decaying vegetation ruled the ground. I used my arms to move blocking branches. I walked against gravity. My heart was pounding and my brain asked, "What is the purpose of this hike?"

"To explore!" exclaimed the deepest fissures of my mind.

Finally, the incline flattened out a bit and I made my way to the left for no particular reason, but to keep going where no one had been before. I saw some boulders and was encouraged by these changes to the understory of this hardwood forest. I walked up the mountain more and more wondering if I was wasting my time or getting myself lost. Why don't I just finish my little exploration hike and go back to the car and eat food, my favorite refuge?

I kept going.

Then I saw a horizontal line biting through the vertical tree trunks. "A cliff," I hoped. I made my way toward the line in the trees. I could see the end of this range of forest stopping and the tops of trees in the distance indicating that something dramatic was coming up. As I got closer, I could see it was a cliff, but would it be an interesting cliff or just a crumbled wall?

The edge dropped straight down with good hard rock. A real cliff – all mine. Hidden far from everything. I was embedded in creation and given a part all my own, which God had made for a day like this when sweat and light were guiding me. I walked along the ridge and was thrilled to see it extended far, but hidden by trees and canopied with an angel's wing. I walked to the base through a crumbly slot and continued to explore. I came across an area where the cliffs curved and made a small amphitheater. How beautiful these rocks appeared. They carried their grays and browns with forceful edges and allowed light to speckle them on occasion. What a wonderful little world. I presumptuously called this area the "Cathedral of the Cliffs" and enjoyed a spot in this troubled world where rocks just stood waiting for me to play and let my imagination wander. Imagination is important. It is part of our ability to create that shows we carry the spark of the divine. Our imagination can layout a delightful roadmap. Einstein said, "Our imagination is our preview of life's coming attractions."

After some moments of immersion, I headed back down the mountain to my car. I knew which way was down, but I wasn't carrying a compass, a GPS, or any other such fickle inventions. After all, I was exploring, and getting lost is part of the adventure. When I got down to the road, I was excited to return with my climbing gear and explore these routes. I have climbed many of the cliffs in this area, and I still go up there without a compass or GPS and discover new faces all the time.

When my kids started moving from childhood years to teenage years, we studied Scripture over many months and then celebrated their growth into maturity. Eric studied Proverbs and Elayna studied the Ten Commandments, the Lord's Prayer, the Epistles, Lydia from Acts, Job, Proverbs 1 and 31, several Psalms, and Romans 8. Each child would sit with me on Sunday nights and we would read and discuss these words of the Lord.

When we were done with these studies, we spent three days together, which culminated with spoken words of deep emotion while we both stood on tiny ledges on a cliff. I found being on a cliff face was the most intimate and otherworldly environment I could share with them. On our celebratory trip, I gave them many sentimental gifts. On the cliffs, I gave them each a knife. I made the knife handles out of tropical hardwood from a decaying Malaysian fishing boat.

For Eric's three days, we went to a cliff where I set up the rappels with two ropes. Then I rappelled down to a ledge where I placed the knife gift. After I had set up everything, Eric and I rappelled down together to the ledge. There I offered words that are lost to the wind and our souls, but I highlighted how I was proud of him and thankful that God would bless me with a son like him. Eric then said, in a precocious manner I thought, his own words of thanks and appreciation. I didn't expect him to have anything to say, but I was impressed that he was moved to say honoring words.

God was closely with us on that cliff. It is a place I have really come to love, where I feel alone with God and nature, held up only by a rope and my wits. You hear a creek rushing below and have a painting of beautiful trees on the other side of the deep valley. Cool rock creates an amphitheater around you and you feel like you are in a special place, sanctified for something. This event I had been planning for months was passing like a wisp of wind through our lives, but it was here, it was now, it was real, it was us, it was love, it was a father and son, it was not a time for tears, but of awe provided by God's kindness. It was a time to notice, to celebrate, to appreciate what God has given us as a father and son. I gave Eric the knife I made him and we clambered up and down the cliff a couple of times. I said he should rappel all by himself; I wasn't even going to watch. He rappelled down in good order and it was done.

I remember saying that there often are times in our lives when we celebrate – births, baptisms, weddings – and less important ones, such as graduations. However, this transition from boyhood to manhood doesn't occur at a certain date; it is a transition, but still one worthy of great notice and celebration.

For Elayna's "blessing on the cliff" weekend, we bushwhacked up to the "cathedral of the cliffs." The ground was wet from the evening's rain, but it helped us dig into the soil as we made our way up the steep, challenging climb with ropes and packs. I prayed that God would give me the right words on the cliff. I was getting nervous that I might not be able to find the cliffs because I seemed to be walking too far. I have always found them by scrambling up until the slope started flattening slightly then bearing left. Maybe on this most important trek to these cliffs I would walk too far or too short to intersect the line of cliffs. With more confused and prayer-drenched plodding, we found them. "Praise the Lord," I thought. We found a brand-new cliff along this line, and there on this untouched cliff I set up a top rope. I rappelled down to test the rig and stored her knife on a ledge on the way down. We rappelled down together on separate ropes and I shared words about my love and God's love as she too slipped the bonds of a dad's tight clutch.

On that ledge, I spoke words of love and joy and we had a moment of grace among the cool rock, the blanket of nature's leaves, the clouds and the heavy air. I don't know what I said exactly, but there were blessings and words from God. I gave her the knife I made, and we rappelled to the bottom and scrambled our way to the top. I was worried that it might rain at any time, so we coiled the ropes and started to leave. We decided to pause at the top where Elayna made a cross in the woods above the cliff. And so ended this precious event, never to be taken away. My love and the blessing offered by God coalesced like a perfect water droplet.

Fear

Climbing has its peculiar set of fears because you don't know how the climb will proceed as you work your way up a cliff. You aren't sure of how good a handhold and foothold you will have as you move up the face of the rock. Conversely, rappelling makes you completely dependent on your equipment and anchor, which should inspire fear.

Having fear is normal. Trusting your life to a rope made by people you don't know and an anchor you created from some fabric attached to aluminum wedges or trees seems to be an act of faith. But it is a faith you can feel and test. Faith in Christ can seem harder because you can't lean back in a safe place and test the belay system – you just walk with spiritual eyes. It seems irrational, but it is the vision of the Holy Spirit that makes the only sense in a senseless world. You fear dying. You fear evil. You fear loneliness and tragedy. None of these concerns can be tested as simply as your belay system. 'What do you really believe?' is a constant refrain in the Christian walk. Our faith is imperfect and by its imperfection we know it is not some bizarre, primal instinct. Our faith is from God and it is challenged by Satan and the world around us. Our faith is not hip or trendy. It can't be explained on a bumper sticker. We are humbled by the ragged, undefined edges of faith, where it meets up with science, common sense, and the gritty world. The ragged edges prove we are not a chemical test tube where boiling temperatures are predictable and replicable. We live in a spiritual world – deal with it. When you are dangling from a rope with nothing but your hand around a rope keeping you from falling, ask yourself *what do you trust in?*

Your courage is drawn upon when you are made vulnerable and out of your controlled environment. While climbing is a matter of personal choice, so is driving to the mall. Which is more dangerous? While Scripture speaks about courage, it is in the context of doing God's will for example in Joshua 1:6-9 and Philippians 1:20. However, courage is commanded in these circumstances, so it is part of our image-bearing of God in humanity. Additionally, we must recognize that courage (as well as all our attributes such as intelligence and strength) comes only from the grace of God.

Many outdoor activities benefit from teamwork, and you have a role in that team. Usually God puts us in communities of some sort, and by His grace we are given gifts that can be used to encourage one another. These gifts are different from our DNA-driven talents.

They come from God, and we are told to recognize and use them (Romans 12). These spiritual gifts allow us to support each other. Spiritual gifts differ from the fruit of the Spirit. This fruit is the purification of our inward character by God.

When contending with outdoor activities, we find a few spiritual gifts that come into prominence, such as service, encouragement and mercy as described in Romans 12:6-8. For example, the ability to show mercy means you can empathize with those struggling in different ways than you. They may be more tired, frightened, or confused than you are, but the divine gift of mercy lets you understand their plight. This is a helpful attribute when working as a group. Likewise, encouragement might mean you don't fully understand someone's challenge, but you can sympathize and encourage him or her forward. The gift of service, being willing to do the physical work needed to accomplish a task, is perhaps the most humble. It is the title that Jesus wanted and should be the title we bear most proudly.

Natural Grace

4

Boating

J.R.R. Tolkien wrote, "Not all those who wander are lost." Recreational boaters are usually wandering. They are not trying to get anywhere – they are just enjoying the water. However, we are not meant to be on the water: we are meant to drink water. Water can be especially frightening, from open horizons of the sea to our rushing, flooded creeks and rivers. I can imagine the faith it took for Peter to walk out to Jesus on the water. To leave the sliver of refuge his boat provided and go out to greet his Lord. That first step – what was that like?

However, water usually provides peaceful refuge and a sense of freedom. Like rock climbing or bushwhacking, you feel you are far from home and in an environment not your own. I have always had a special fondness for the water. The open horizons of the ocean and large lakes draw me out.

When I was about 13, I took a rowboat across a lake to get blueberries. I thought there was going to be a storm and I was afraid of being hit by lightning. I rowed quickly back to our campground and told my mom my worries about the weather. My mom and dad emigrated from the west coast of Norway soon after they were married and knew the sea well. My mom said that you could feel the weather ahead of time on the water. She was right (aren't moms always right?). You learn quickly the relationship between the wind, the movement of the water, the clouds, and the sunlight. Reading water and feeling wind lets you sail as naturally as riding a bike.

I have enjoyed chartering boats, usually out of Florida, for many years. When Eric was a couple of years old, we would go to Mt. Pisgah State Park and rent a paddleboat. It was a lot of fun and we felt safe and secure on that beautiful, little lake. Later, I got a small inflatable raft. This was a humbling descent from what I had done in the past. But this raft, which Elayna named Danielle, has given me more joy than any other boat I have owned or operated. We would take it to Rose Valley Lake and explore without the complications of docking, anchoring, or any of the other encumbering requirements of handling a large boat. We would plow into cattails and see what was alive on the stems and in the murky water. We would beach onto every shoreline and explore the sand and rocks. We fell out the boat and swam around it. We even had a fish flop into our boat having been lifted up by our paddle.

The best part of the raft was how we would all pile on top of each other so it was like a family wresting match. I would sit at one end with my legs out, and Eric and Elayna would sit on my legs. We were low in the water and could flop in and out easily. It was always half swimming and half boating.

When Eric was seven years old, he took on the challenge of rowing it by himself from shore to shore. It was a lot of work and it satisfied the daring-do of a young boy. However, I realized my family was outgrowing this little raft, so I built a wooden skiff that Elayna named "Cornelia." I would lay awake at night thinking about the boatbuilding tasks that needed to be done and their optimal sequence. This type of work really gets into my blood. We christened her with milk and she replaced our dear inflatable raft. Everyone could fit into all 13 feet of Cornelia, including Beth. I loved the sound of the wood. Maybe all boats should be made out of wood?

I later converted her to a sailboat by adding a piece of electrical conduit and a bottom, sole plate made from a cast iron flange fitting. I used a plastic tarp for a sail. It could only go downwind, but it was nice to have some kind of sailing craft in the fleet.

You don't get many big adventures in a rowboat. The closest thing we got was when we went out on a very windy day with the bow slapping against the steep little waves. Coming back against the wind required me to row with all my strength and go from point to point along the shore so I could rest up for the next frantic rowing segment. With her flat bottom, Cornelia was easy to beach, but she had high sides, so we couldn't just roll out of the boat as we could with the raft. Our half-submerged raft was replaced with a floating park bench.

In order to explore the waterways better, I designed and built a small canoe with a clear bottom panel. It also had a hole in the bottom with a riser pipe so I could lower things and grab things in the water. It had a metal bowsprit, skid plates, and mounts for attaching to Cornelia. It had a hand-drawn face at the bow to complete the whimsical work. I made it from one sheet of 3/8 inch plywood and leftover fiberglass and epoxy. It was ugly. We called her the 'Bounty Hunter,' and Elayna and I enjoyed watching streambeds and crayfish through her acrylic window. She was a poor man's submarine that was fun to create.

Creating from our imagination lies in the domain of humans. We can take what is around us and create something new, whether it is a glass-bottom boat or a painting. More than merely a spark of the divine, we are image bearers of Christ, which is shown in our ability to create. I am thankful that God has gifted us with this ability.

Cutting wood, driving screws, applying epoxy, and all the other tasks involved with boat building can glorify God. Colossians 3 says that we should work as if we are working for the Lord. Many of the things I have described can be thought of as fun, self-centered, or ego-driven adventures. Unlike these playful forays, work and creation are blessed actions. God values work. With the fall of man, God did not curse work, He cursed the ground. The cursed ground and corrupted nature remind of us a future glory where death is gone and all is as it should be. When we work, we can bring glory to God with our worn fingertips and tired minds. Work is not bad; it is something we give to God. We are creators and we rule over God's creation with providential gifts. We are deeply called to co-create.

A few years after making the wooden boats, I bought an ancient Sunfish sailboat. The Sunfish is a sailing scow, meaning it is flat-bottomed, fast, and tipsy (or 'tender' in sailor's parlance). If you can sail a Sunfish you can sail anything – it is less forgiving than the 40-footers I used to charter. I loved racing across the lake with the "Thelma H." (named after Beth's grandmother). The big problem with sailboats is they are a pain to set up. I always make mistakes. But once rigged and in deep water, they are one of the most wonderful machines available. Sailboats carry you with nature's breath wherever you aim your tiller.

Eric would want to go out in crazy winds. Because you can't reduce the sail on a Sunfish, you basically have an on/off switch. In strong winds, you can easily bring her up on plane, which provides a thrilling ride while water foams and rages around the hull. Going upwind, you can only depower the sail by stalling the back of the sail slightly. This luffing keeps the tender boat from tipping over.

This out of control sailing is scary and I prefer more calm wind for this little boat. Large keelboats are fun in big winds because you can reduce the sails in a controlled way, and the hulls have heavy keels that make them self-righting. However, you get a great feel for the wind and water on a small boat.

One time, Elayna and I were exploring all the little nooks we liked at Rose Valley Lake under perfect summer conditions – you can't beat our area's weather in the summer. As we were slowly making our way back to shore, I hit a submerged stump with the centerboard. We lurched forward a bit, but it was a gentle bump with no damage. However, it was completely unexpected and for those few moments where your upper body was traveling faster than the rest of your body, it was confusing. I told Elayna it was another smile from Jesus so that we would remember our time together sailing on this perfect summer day – an exclamation point provided by an old submerged stump. "Never would it have a grander purpose," I thought as I metaphorically threw it into the Russian fireplace. We all love a little surprise. Not too much to be frightened – just enough to get our blood flowing.

There are many other beautiful waters in our area, from the powerful Susquehanna River to the placid mountain lakes. We have especially enjoyed Steven Foster Lake at Mt. Pisgah State Park. When Eric was small, we would go there and rent a paddleboat. We had great fun in this energy-consuming, inefficient device. We wouldn't get far, but we were out in the water and Eric could use every bit of his energy without harm. When Elayna was older, we kayaked there a couple of times. Kayaking is a lot fun because you are low in the water, reasonably stable, and highly maneuverable. You can sneak into shores and quickly make your way through the water. Once we went out right after a storm, so we had the lake to ourselves, and when we returned from our little foray, we were greeted with a beautiful rainbow. Another smile from Jesus. We even watched a bird fly right under the apex of the rainbow. Who could make a better painting?

Assurance

While the rainbow is a reminder of God's promise to Noah that God would not flood the world again, we must be on guard that we don't seek clues from nature to provide us assurance of salvation. We won't find this assurance of salvation in people or rituals either.

In nature, truth drives consequences very directly. If it is cold outside, you will get cold, if it is wet you will get wet. You can't talk yourself out of these consequences. There is no hypocrisy in these interactions.

We can't handle hypocrites – and the church is full of them. You encounter people who carry the name "Christian" when it is comfortable and something else when it's not. Is the term "Christian" an indicator of faith or culture? The church is full of frustrated sinners who are angry with themselves. We say one thing, yet do something else. We have anger, shame, and doubt. We don't completely accept God's forgiveness and we carry shame and lies. Most of us run through a cycle of sinning, repentance, and forgiveness. This cycle is like spitting in your parent's face when he or she gives you a hug. Being a Christian is not about rules, but relationships. Part of that relationship is understanding how God talks to you through the Bible.

All humans are spiritual. We can have our mood altered by music and environments, but a relationship requires understanding and love. The understanding comes from the Bible, and Christian love comes from the Holy Spirit. It is our love for one another that God considers the second greatest commandment (with loving God being the greatest). Nature fails our Christian walk completely in this regard. Trees do not create relationships – only people do. It is for this reason we gather with believers so that we might encourage one another. So how do we develop this relationship with God? We read the Bible and use other means of grace such as prayer, preaching, and the Sacraments.

We are assured of our salvation by recognizing the fruit of the Spirit. These are specific gifts God gives us that glorify Him and provide evidence of our salvation. The most important fruit is probably the desire to love others as described in John 13:35: "All people will know that you are my disciples, if you have love for one another." Jesus goes on to say in John 14:15 that loving Jesus also means keeping His commandments. Paul offers a concise list of attitudes that ensure our calling and salvation: "The fruit of the Spirit is love, joy, peace, patience, kindness, goodness, faithfulness, gentleness, self-control" (Galatians 5:22). Paul goes on to write in Galatians 5:25, "If we live by the Spirit, let us also keep in step with the Spirit."

Does being "born again" sound like a precursor to snake handling and weird religions? Being born again means being regenerated by the Holy Spirit so that Christ is in you in a manner that is personal and real. You then become spiritually reborn. This is a common Biblical term and it comes from the notion of being adopted into the kingdom of God.

We don't remember when we were physically born, yet we know we are alive by the physical and mental operations of our body. In the same manner, if you don't recall when you were spiritually born again, you can still know you are spiritually alive by spiritual fruit. The fruit of salvation is an ongoing blessing that parallels our physical birth by showing the operation of the Holy Spirit in us. Therefore, we mustn't carry our conversion experience as our assurance of salvation but rather the ongoing fruit of the Spirit as shown in our thoughts and actions. This fruit was described in Galatians 5:22 previously. We are judged by our fruit, not by having our socks knocked off some years ago.

People have different experiences coming to faith. Some are blessed like Paul, who saw a light brighter than the sun and was given a commission to do exactly the opposite of what he was doing – namely stop persecuting Christians and preach to the Gentiles. Paul was also blinded for three days to make clear the power of Christ.

In contrast, the cloth merchant, Lydia, responded to Paul's presentation of the gospel message as follows:

The Lord opened her heart to pay attention to what was said by Paul. And after she was baptized, and her household as well, she urged us, saying, "If you have judged me to be faithful to the Lord, come to my house and stay." (Acts 16:14b-15a)

She seems to have had a less dramatic change than Paul, but one that led her to act by both baptizing her family and offering Christian hospitality.

Many are brought to faith at a young age as covenant children. Our closeness to God develops in an ongoing process. This is how the people of Israel came to be God's people, by a covenant not drama.

God gives us faith and His work in our salvation can take many twists. We pray in the Lord's Prayer specifically not to be led into temptation. But God allows temptations for His own purposes. If we love Jesus as a child, then seemingly walk away from Him for a time, and then recover our love for Him, were we not Christians as a child? What was this walk in darkness?

Our Christian walk can include times when we are left to temptations and corruptions. Sin is still sin, but God uses everything, including these fallen times, for His own purposes. We should look for these purposes. Maybe we will be able to identify the purpose for backsliding.[1] These purposes may be to amplify our understanding of His grace, to humble us, or to discipline us. These times when we were far from God can help us show God's grace by loving people when they are also blinded to their sin. We can't be spectators to grace, we have to recognize God's grace in our own lives so that we might appreciate it and live as redeemed and recovered people.

Regardless of the conversion experience, we know that nothing can separate us from Christ. We are sealed for salvation as clearly described by Paul in Romans 8:35-39:

> Who shall separate us from the love of Christ? Shall tribulation, or distress, or persecution, or famine, or nakedness, or danger, or sword? As it is written, "For your sake we are being killed all the day long; we are regarded as sheep to be slaughtered."

> No, in all these things we are more than conquerors through him who loved us. For I am sure that neither death nor life, nor angels nor rulers, nor things present nor things to come, nor powers, nor height nor depth, nor anything else in all creation, will be able to separate us from the love of God in Christ Jesus our Lord.

God always initiates conversion. We are declared righteous by God and given the full rights of God's people described all the way back in Genesis. We are

22

given the Holy Spirit to live in us and help us be more like Jesus. This process of sanctification leads us to make Jesus' thoughts our thoughts also. Ephesians 5:8-10 describes this deeply-rooted change in attitude: "For at one time you were darkness, but now you are light in the Lord. Walk as children of light (for the fruit of light is found in all that is good and right and true), and try to discern what is pleasing to the Lord." These changes then motivate us to act in God-pleasing ways. Ephesians 5:1-2 makes this clear, "Therefore be imitators of God, as beloved children. And walk in love, as Christ loved us and gave himself up for us, a fragrant offering and sacrifice to God."

Mark Talbot, a philosophy professor at Wheaton College, offered this breakdown of questions that reflect on how we respond to salvation. He calls it a "preliminary test."

1. Have you heard God's Word proclaimed?
2. Does your life show signs of true repentance?
3. Have you deliberately and decisively turned from living a life enslaved to sin to living a life that takes Christ to be both your Savior and your Lord?
4. Do you find your heart to have been changed so that you now want to follow God's decrees and keep his laws?[2]

However, God is sovereign, and some may not hear "the Word proclaimed" in a way we understand and still be saved. Those with mental or physical handicaps may learn of God's Word through means that God chooses. However, the normal sequence of salvation is in response to hearing or reading the gospel message.

Martin Luther wrote much about what faith means in the day-to-day life of the believer. He observed the dichotomy of an "easy", passive access to salvation and our active response to it, noting, "A Christian man is the most free lord of all, and subject to none; a Christian man is the most dutiful servant of all, and subject to every one."[3]

There are physical responses to faith. In James 2:17, the author writes, "So also faith by itself, if it does not have works, is dead." However, our response is more a heart attitude that drives actions rather than the physical acts that we crave to "prove" our faith and ensure our salvation. Our heart attitudes are fickle and difficult to discern. It is much easier to light a candle or go through some ceremony than give our hearts fully to Christ.

5

Downhill Skiing

Snow has always been a playground for me. I have loved the first snow of the season since I was a little child. Not only is everything beautiful but it is slippery, moldable, and all around fun. Snow forts and sledding are only moments away. I used to celebrate the first snowfall of the season with my kids with a bare-footed, shirtless backyard wrestling match. We would spend New Year's Eve night sleeping outside in the backyard to toughen us for the coming year. Snow gives me a short window to play like a kid, enjoy deep silence, interpret the story of fresh animal tracks – and ski.

As I write this, Elayna and I went outside into the gulley behind our house to enjoy the fresh snowfall. After enjoying this well-worn part of our world and its dialogue of deer tracks, we sat at the base of a tree and waited for the moon to rise. It takes a while for the moon to work its way through the gray trunks, but it got brighter and the edges could be seen. I started singing the song "Sing Hallelujah to the Lord" and Elayna sang the harmony in our well-practices tradition.

When we have a good Nor'easter, lie on your back in deep snow and watch the trees above you swirl in the wind. The tops of the trees pierce into the sky, making a complex array of lines reminding me of the capillaries in the back of my eye when I get an eye exam. The movement of the branches is disorienting and magical. When you lay in the snow, it hugs your body, and it is reassuring and incredibly comfortable.

I never taught anyone how to ski. Actually, I was never really taught. When I was in college, a friend at work graciously asked me if I wanted to ski and he taught me some basics. After that, I just read books and experimented, which is how I have learned many of my outdoor skills. The icy slopes of Indiana and old-fashioned skis helped me develop good edging techniques for parallel turns. When Eric was eight years old, I thought it was a good time to get him downhill skiing. With modern, shaped skis and groomed trails at Ski Sawmill it was much more fun and controlled than the last time I had skied over ten years prior. It was like driving a Ferrari. And when I bought my first set of downhill skis, I was in heaven. No more waiting in rental lines and wearing undersized boots that caused bloody toes.

I have many sad stories from my early years of skiing. Bloody toes, icy wipeouts, long lift lines, stupidly long car drives, and even a case after the Sarajevo Olympics where they didn't have boots my size and I had to just walk around in the deep snow waiting for my friends to finish skiing. I won't linger on that too much; I guess the equipment-centric and expensive world of skiing still stings my memory.

However, in our area we have access to great, family-friendly ski slopes with short lift lines, decent snow, and peaceful settings. When I taught Eric to ski, I was starting with no formal techniques or approaches. I brought a rope to tie to him and stuck it in my pocket. I thought I would just teach him to snow plow and see how it progressed. As it turns out, dealing with kids and ski equipment is a real challenge. It seemed to take forever before we got to the lift line. Then we had to deal with a tow bar, which presents all sorts of challenges to a new skier, with us wiping out the first time we tried to alight. We picked up our fallen skis and bodies and walked from under the tow rope. We made our way past the onlookers to the back of the line – humiliation and punishment of its own kind. We put on our skis and things went better from there. We had a great first ski experience, and I brought chocolate and other treats because I wanted this to be a fun-filled, memorable day.

Eric learned quickly and loved it. His low center of gravity and lack of fear let him progress rapidly. By the third time out, he was going down the steep, black diamond slope and I couldn't catch up. It is a unique transition to go from a doting and protective dad to a prayerful watcher. Soon Elayna was also learning to ski and quickly became a confident skier.

The best part of the ski trips were the ski lifts. We would talk about our last ski run, then talk about all sorts of random and delightfully peaceful topics as our feet dangled and we cocooned in another world, just the two of us. We practiced saying hard words like 'onomatopoeia' and 'Teotihuacan' and described the unique squeaking sounds of our chair. We talked about school, work, people, and dreams while waiting for our next flight on snow.

I also enjoyed resting in the parking lot. I would take off my skis, sit in the car, and pull out the food Beth made for me. Then I would listen to a Christian radio station and write in my journal. If I was with the kids, we would relax and talk. We could sit right at the foot of the mountain, no transfer bus, no pretense. Just walk in the frozen gravel parking lot and have a picnic in your car. Nothing like hot cocoa, tired legs, and cold air to make you feel cozy in a car. I would be at peace and pour out my love for what Christ gave me in my notebook. This is a unique aspect of downhill skiing compared to other outdoor activities. You can toggle between flying on the snow to comfortable seats and good food in minutes.

The kids started many outdoor activities when they were eight years old. Eight is a good age to introduce the adventures that lie in our area. Kids are moving from a delightfully playful stage to one where they wish to test their abilities and find out what they can do.

Waiting

The snow subdues sound. It cushions the ground and absorbs the distant birdcalls. The silence of snow can be magical, and it can let the mind race. We can't seem to stop our mind. It is difficult to place the focus of our mind on a single point and let it meditate. Archery and math are good at focusing the mind and pushing back the noise. But where should our minds go when things are silent? Waiting for the Lord can seem like silence. When we are in a difficult time in our lives, the future seems too far away. Waiting seems like crawling through tangled weeds, you just want to jump over them. The Bible guides us saying, "They who wait for the Lord shall renew their strength" (Isaiah 40:31) and

"Blessed is the man who listens to me, watching daily at my gates, waiting beside my doors" (Proverbs 8:34). This is tough when the world seems ugly and lonely – when God seems far away. It is times like this we need to be close to God through prayer and Bible study – and be still. When I am agitated, the last thing I want to do is read the Bible and be still. This is part of the challenge to the Christian walk. It is not always a time of praise songs and candles. It can be a walk of anger, frustration, and conflict. We seek peace of mind and we wait for God's timing.

Perhaps we can become too much at peace. David was very concerned with this. He highlights his battle with complacency in the Psalms (for example Psalm 26, 119, and 139). David asks that his heart be searched and he be taught God's will: "Search me, O God, and know my heart!" (Psalm 139:23).

David knows he is loved by God, but wants to improve his obedience. He asks that he not just accept his current state, but that God will reveal things that David doesn't want to know so that he can be more Christ-like.

David is one of many figures in the Bible who had long periods of waiting and deep distress until their purpose was clear. Moses, Joseph, and the apostles are some of the notable figures that endured periods of loneliness, slavery, and imprisonment until they were in circumstances where they could take actions that obviously promoted the Gospel. While Paul was a prisoner in Rome, he made sense of his troubles, stating: "that what has happened to me has actually served to advance the gospel. As a result, it has become clear throughout the whole imperial guard and to all the rest that my imprisonment is for Christ" (Philippians 1:12b-13). We must ask how our difficult circumstances serve God, and how they are filling His agenda.

Charles Spurgeon writes that waiting on the Lord is part of the walk, but there will be an end to the waiting.

> "If you want to serve God and cannot find the favorable occasion, wait awhile in prayer, and your opportunity will break on your path like a sunbeam.... Every diligent laborer is needed in some part of His vineyard. You may have to linger; you may seem as if you stood in the market idle because the Master would not engage you; but wait there in prayer and with your heart boiling over with a warm purpose, and your chance will come."[1]

Natural Grace

6

Cross Country Skiing

I have been cross-country skiing since I was a boy. I remember my mom calling me when I was working on building a ham radio in the basement, asking me if I wanted to go skiing. We never did things like that, so it was a real thrill. We rented skis and I fell in love with this efficient way of moving through the snow. When I was young, it seemed I could ski forever. Or perhaps that is just romantic memory.

There are great places to ski in our area, from the commercial, groomed trails to bushwalking through the small grassy parks. My favorite is Rider Park because it is close and free – two big priorities for me. Cross-country skiing is easy to do and it can get you in great physical shape. It doesn't have the thrill of downhill skiing, but it lets you move beautifully through our woods. And all this exercise makes food taste better, warm drinks feel richer, and your bed feel more comfortable.

Sometimes when making new tracks, my skis are under the snow with just a suggestion of a ski tip near the surface. This seems funny to me, as if I'm skiing underground. But then my ankle breaks through the snow and I see a nice, groomed trail in my wake. The easy sliding motion makes me appreciate the blanket of snow that smoothes out all the rocks and roots. Skiing takes away the ankle dancing that occurs when walking on trails. Skiing seems too easy, as if I am cheating or something. However, it isn't the most social activity. The scratching snow makes noise and it is hard to hear the person in front of you or behind you. But there is a strange mixture of stark silence and ski swooshes reminding me of how I am disturbing the peace.

I only use the diagonal stride technique where you kick back your leg to move forward. This engages the sticky wax or herringbone pattern on the bottom the ski with the snow and lets you push off with your other leg. Skating is a newer technique that uses shorter skis, and you use the edge of your skis to give you engagement with the snow. This technique seems to work only on prepared surfaces. With diagonal striding, you can work through fresh snow, but it is much faster and easier when you can go on existing tracks.

Cross-country skiing gives you time to think about things. You are usually following a trail; the woods are quiet except for your swooshing metronome of skis. I look at the blue sky etched with leafless trees and think, "What is all this made from?"

When our body moves like a graceful machine and we are propelled through woods and fields, there is a beauty of the mechanical machine that God made in our bodies. Where muscles talk to bones, and blood feeds the fire of motion. We are raw, fast temples of our Father deeply drawing in His air and streaming through His beautiful, icy wilderness.

Prayer

Can you pray while you are skiing? Does God demand that you stop and fall on your knees and enter a special state of transcendence?

How to pray is something with which I struggle. In Scripture, prayers range from the all night, heart-wrenching communion of Jesus in Gethsemane to the brief prayer for prosperity of Jabez. Because God knows our thoughts (Romans 8:26) we may wonder, "Why pray?" One answer could be we are commanded to pray (and pray without ceasing), and the other is to nurture ourselves with a communion with Christ.

We know from Jesus' guidance in the Lord's Prayer that we are to pray for God's 'will to be done.' That is the fundamental prayer. In John 14:14, Jesus says, "If you ask me anything in my name, I will do it." But this is in the context of our desire to glorify God, and it involves a deeper notion of praying in "my name" actually means. "My name" means you recognize the essence of who Jesus is and pray in that regard. While Jesus acts as our priest in speaking to the Father, it is the prayers that are in accordance with His will that are honored. However, we are admonished to pray without ceasing (1 Thessalonians 5:17). Short breath or exclamatory prayers of "God help me"; "God be with me"; "Praise the Lord" are the most intimate and powerful for me.

The prophet Nehemiah was very anxious when he was addressed by the Persian king Artaxerxes. Therefore, Nehemiah paused for the briefest time to pray to God. It was so brief, the king didn't seem to notice, as you can see in the following description of events:

> "The king said to me, "What is it you want?" Then I prayed to the God of heaven, and I answered the king" (Nehemiah 2:4-5a).

It is a delightful sequence of priorities to see that the lowly Nehemiah addressed his God before addressing his king.

Prayers of praise are awkward for me. Just handing over your list of wants to God is like visiting a family member that only asks you for favors without any other mix in the conversation. Thankfully, God has given us the Psalms, which contain many praise songs. Reciting praise verses from Scripture shouldn't be ritualistic. However, praising God with Scripture is acceptable worship.

Besides praying back God's praise, the Bible can guide our prayer. For example, when Psalm 119:37-38 says:

Turn my eyes from looking at worthless things;
And give me life in your ways.
Confirm to your servant your promise,
that you may be feared.

This becomes a prayer such as: "Lord, let me not put material things and idolatrous thoughts ahead of you. Strengthen my faith and give me assurance of salvation."

This Psalm 119-derived prayer is requesting things – supplications. Praying can be richly organized around the structure of 1) adoration, 2) confession, 3) thanksgiving, and 4) supplication. A helpful acrostic to recall this structure is 'ACTS'. This organization encourages us to firstly, say how we love God for who He is and not what He has done for us (adoration). Secondly, we should confess our sins and be contrite about how we have offended God's holiness (confession). Thirdly, we thank God for what He has done for us, such as being able to hide behind Jesus' righteousness! We also thank God for other things, such as our food, family, and faith (thanksgiving). The final element (supplication), is asking God for stuff. This is a portion of prayer when we ask God for things. It is easy to dwell in this last step.

This structure of prayer helps me remember I am approaching a holy God and I am quivering behind Jesus as I ask Him to help me out with my troubles. Compare this approach with that of the Old Testament priests. They had to make all sorts of dramatic physical preparations before approaching God.

Jesus presented the Lord's Prayer during the Sermon on the Mount in Matthew 5 and 6. Jesus says in Matthew 6:9-13 the following:

> Pray then like this:
> Our Father in heaven,
> hallowed be your name.
> Your kingdom come,

your will be done,
on earth as it is in heaven.
Give us this day our daily bread,
and forgive us our debts,
as we also have forgiven our debtors.
And lead us not into temptation,
but deliver us from evil.

Adoration is shown with "hallowed be your name." Confession is indicated in the prayer "forgive us our debts." Supplication is shown with the requests for "our day," "daily bread," "lead us not into temptation," and "deliver us from evil." Thanksgiving is not directly addressed here, but we are to be thankful as Paul taught in Philippians 4:6: "Do not be anxious about anything, but in everything by prayer and supplication with thanksgiving let your requests be made known to God." There is a cycle between asking for things and thanking God for these things.

Natural Grace

7

Caving

As with skiing, I started caving (spelunking) in the Midwest. Southern Indiana, where I worked as a student engineer at Cummins Engine Company, has rich swaths of beautifully clear limestone. Towns carrying geological names such as Ollitic (as in ollitic limestone) lie above a labyrinth of caves. In one part of the Blue Springs cavern, a friend and I would float on inner tubes as far as we could before crawling through cold mud to explore areas that no one had visited. I was also part of a spelunking club that would map caves. Several of the caves in that area had never been explored, but these wild caves were not particularly beautiful and hours of being wet and cold really challenged my enthusiasm. Dining on smooshed peanut butter sandwiches didn't help either.

In our area, we have some caves, but they have been explored and are well-used. One cave in Centre County allowed Elayna and I plus some other friends who had experience in this cave to explore God's unique creation. The notion of a world under our world seems to draw out a deep desire for exploration. While not a parallel world or journey to the center of the earth by any measure, it seems delightfully mysterious to squeeze through subterranean cracks that test both your claustrophobia and your fear of getting stuck in a squeezing passage. Squirming through a passage produces a unique type of fear – one that I don't encounter anywhere else. Overcoming fear is a special challenge when the fear is rooted in pure exploration (or perhaps recreation?) rather than pursuing some tangible goal. The fear illustrates our physical and mental vulnerability and lack of real security in this fallen world.

Like rock climbing and boating, caving puts you where you don't belong. However, unlike rock climbing, you are completely cocooned in rock while caving. As I squeeze through holes, I feel cozy and frightened. My delicate ribs and dependence on small chest movements to breathe seem dangerously opposed to the hard rocks around me. However, entering into large openings is a beautiful experience.

Caving lets you appreciate the sky and the reassurance it provides. You know where you belong, and that is not in a small underground tunnel. Perhaps that is why the notion of hell seems to have this feature. Dante's ninth circle of hell is at the most remote spot away from the familiar surface of the earth. While Satan chews on Judas, Brutus, and Cassius, they are surrounded by rock and fire, and expelled from the beautiful sky that we call our home. When Virgil and Dante emerge from their tour, they richly appreciate the sky:

> My guide and I did enter, to return
> To the fair world: and heedless of repose
> We climb'd, he first, I following his steps,
> Till on our view the beautiful lights of heaven
> Dawn'd through a circular opening in the cave;
> Then issuing we again beheld the stars.[1]

There is a certain ghoulishness to being underground and in the dark. I think of H.P. Lovecraft's rich description of his underground approach to the Martense's haunted house through tunnels:

> What language can describe the spectacle of a man lost in infinitely abysmal earth; pawing, twisting, wheezing; scrambling madly through sunken convolutions of immemorial blackness without an idea of time, safety, direction, or definite object? There is something hideous in it, but that is what I did. I did it for so long that life

faded to a far memory, and I became one with the moles and grubs of nighted depths.[2]

Evil

Lovecraft finds mutilated bodies under the earth in the Catskill Mountains of upstate New York. This reminds me of the evil surrounding us and the old question, "Why do bad things happen to good people?" If you search Scripture, you see that no one is good. As you dig further, you see that God doesn't need to report to you and explain His reasoning.

For example, in Job 38:2-4, God replies to Job's ongoing questioning about why his life has been ruined, simply as follows:

> Who is this that darkens counsel by words without knowledge?
> Dress for action like a man;
> I will question you, and you make it known to me.
> Where were you when I laid the foundation of the earth?
> Tell me, if you have understanding.

This was in response to Job's ongoing declarations of self-righteousness. He was not broken to his sins, but compared himself to others.

God doesn't seem to give an answer that satisfies us. He simply says He is our Lord. Some things He lets us understand and some things He doesn't. You learn about this feature of God's plan in Deuteronomy 29:29, where God decrees, "The secret things belong to the LORD our God, but the things that are revealed belong to us and to our children forever, that we may do all the words of this law."

Furthermore, in Isaiah 55:8-9 we read:

For my thoughts are not your thoughts,
neither are your ways my ways, declares the
LORD.
For as the heavens are higher than the earth,
so are my ways higher than your ways
and my thoughts than your thoughts.

In Romans chapter 9, Paul states that God is sovereign, and in our fallen condition, God will decide whom to have mercy upon. Paul uses the metaphor of the pot versus the pot maker in Romans 9:22: "Has the potter no right over the clay, to make out of the same lump one vessel for honorable use and another for dishonorable use?"

Jesus' mission was not to fulfill you personally, but to be the Lord of the universal church — all creation and all nations. We must rely on faith, not feelings, and recall that God permits and limits our suffering.

Paul dealt with the battle between evil, God's will, and our own weakness:

So I find it to be a law that when I want to do right, evil lies close at hand. For I delight in the law of God, in my inner being, but I see in my members another law waging war against the law of my mind and making me captive to the law of sin that dwells in my members. Wretched man that I am! Who will deliver me from this body of death? Thanks be to God through Jesus Christ our Lord! So then, I myself serve the law of God with my mind, but with my flesh I serve the law of sin. (Romans 7:21-26)

However, the good news is that our suffering lets us share the cross with Jesus. And while suffering resulted from the fall of Adam, the challenges we face will glorify God, and our response to these challenges allow us to grow closer to God. As Paul writes in James 1, "Count it all joy, my brothers, when you meet trials of various kinds, for you know that the testing of your faith produces steadfastness. And let steadfastness have its full effect, that you may be perfect and complete, lacking in nothing."

Psalm 73 notes the challenge of living in a world where the evil often get ahead in society. Broken rules seem to win the day.

For I was envious of the arrogant
when I saw the prosperity of the wicked.

For they have no pangs until death;
their bodies are fat and sleek.
They are not in trouble as others are;
they are not stricken like the rest of mankind.
(Psalm 73:3-5)

But are these "rule breakers" at peace when they lay their heads down at night? Psalm 73 continues:

Truly you set them in slippery places;
you make them fall to ruin.
How they are destroyed in a moment,
swept away utterly by terrors!
Like a dream when one awakes,
O Lord, when you rouse yourself,
you despise them as phantoms.
(Psalm 73:18-25)

Natural Grace

8

Camping

Camping is hearth and home brought to the forest's edge. When I was a child, our family camping trips were the highlight of the year. We would go once a year when my dad (and later my mom) earned a little vacation. We would pile into our sedan and drive to a campground. There we would set up the world's largest canvas tent for our family of seven and eat Spam and sandwiches. Playing, fishing, and exploring were all the activities for the day. Each day would end with the magic of a campfire and cozy sleeping arrangements. These camping trips drew out every joy a young boy could possess.

There are so many great places to camp in our area that favorites seem to derive more from tradition than quality. We blend swimming and walking with trips to McDonalds and driving adventures. Camping is a great way to mix healthy nature hikes with s'mores and campfire smoke. Camping is very social and makes you appreciate your home and all its conveniences. Camping lets you spend time doing things you never seem to do otherwise, like playing games and enjoying long conversations.

During the day, camping lets us take meandering walks and build sandcastles while basking in that sneaky feeling of being 'away from home.' At night, camping gives us time to lie down and watch the Perseid meteor shower and International Space Station. It lets us stare at a campfire and enjoy random conversations. We develop great camaraderie when surrounded by lurking darkness and black skies. The stars are beautiful but make us feel tiny and overwhelmed.

Camping is all about attitude. If you go in not liking it, you will leave in worst shape. However, it offers a platform for great conversations while washed with summer wind and soothing leaf rustles. You can go heavy with gear and food. You have an escape vehicle and real bathrooms.

I have spent an embarrassing amount of time in tents. I lived in one all summer in college to save money, and when I was working on a seismic exploration team in Venezuela. I have "camped" while traveling many times. But this isn't the fun camping we are talking about here.

I have had other funny things happen while camping, but it usually involves rain, which I guess is not that funny. However, camping makes for a cheap hotel if nothing else, and it keeps you close to nature. It can provide its own creature comforts. Helen Keller opined, "To me a lush carpet of pine needles or spongy grass is more welcome than the most luxurious Persian rug." Camping is sort of the beach for our area. You can sit and read a book without feeling guilty about some task at home you should be working on.

Camping is a great experience for all generations. It is often children's first immersion in nature. Camping offers a delightful bookend in your senior years because you can drag what you need with you and move out of the tent into something nicer.

Even though nature provides a cozy space, we must remember that worshiping alone in the woods is not a Scriptural approach to worship. Worship is administered by human agents and by those called to these responsibilities.

The Bible

Reading for enjoyment is one of the benefits of camping. It gives us quality time to read and mediate on Scripture. The Bible presents theological reality and the history of salvation. It is not a science book, but inspired words telling of God's plan for our salvation. The Bible presents a consistent testimony of God's plan for the redemption and restoration of humanity. This salvation history extends from creation and the fall of Adam to the incarnate Christ and His church.

The Bible shows the faults of leaders and those normally in charge of written history. Think of how David's sin is condemned all the way into the New Testament's presentation of Jesus' genealogy. In Matthew 1, David's son, Solomon, is noted as being born by "the wife of Uriah". This is remarkable. What ancient writings keep records of failures of rulers? Even with more modern writing, we recognize that "history is a fable agreed upon by the victors," to paraphrase Napoleon. I'm a broken sinner full of faults and a long list of mistakes, but I don't include these mistakes in this writing for your review. I hide them to history.

Many stories in the Bible seem strange, and it can feel anti-intellectual to believe them. These stories need to be considered in the context of God's holiness, hatred of sin, special care for His people, and plan for their redemption. Some of these stories make my jaw drop in confusion or disgust. They make me wonder, "What is going on here?" If you don't consider these underlying truths, you will get stopped at descriptions of such events as the flood with which Noah contended, the parting of the Red Sea, and the destruction of the Canaanites, to name a few. These stories show God's power and willingness to judge evil. It reminds us that the consequence of sin is death (Genesis 2:17). We are addicted to sin and suppress truth. We idolize God's blessings and make them gods. However, the Bible constantly reminds us that God would not let our sin take over our lives and God has a plan to overrule sin through Christ.

There are many great books that describe the accuracy of the Bible and commentaries that offer excellent insights into challenging parts of the Bible (see Suggested Reading). If some verse or story is offensive or confusing, please consult these resources. Remember Jesus said the greatest commandments were to love God and love your neighbor. This is the context for all the ostensibly bothersome stories you might encounter in the Bible. Avoiding the tough stories is why many huddle around the Sermon on the Mount (Matthew 5-7) and other approachable New Testament didactic presentations. However, the Old Testament points to the incarnate Jesus and is an important source for a systematic theology.

Your reason and intellect need to contend with the question, "What do I believe?" Do I trust the Bible, or is there something more reliable? If there is something else, what is it? Science perhaps? What is science and how does science contend with issues that can't be measured – the transcendent? Do I trust my intuition? What is intuition? Questions and more questions. But you have to consider these questions to establish a worldview that emboldens your life. Otherwise, you will strive to get distracted from real issues by engaging the entertainment and distraction culture that seeks to occupy every gap in your time. Playing a video game replaces reflection; an inane flow of social media replaces introspection.

The Bible lets us know God better. It describes His attributes and purposes and the history of salvation. When reading the Bible, constantly consider how the reading tells you more about Jesus Christ. For example, the escape from slavery in Egypt is about redemption for sin. The massive killings are about God's holiness and His hatred toward sin. Consider the unity of the Bible. The story of redemption through Jesus is woven across many authors, times, and locations.

Nature follows laws. These natural laws have been an area of study for millennia. Why does nature operate as it does? Nature is governed by laws ranging from gravity to thermodynamics. Humans don't claim to be above these laws, but many of us also submit to moral laws, from the Hindu's Upanishads to the Ten Commandments. We further submit to the laws of our government and perhaps the values of our favorite entertainment personality.

Christians submit to God's moral laws. These loving admonishments are presented and clarified from Genesis to Revelation. God's moral law is crystallized by the Ten Commandments. Finally, we need to recognize God has the final word on the authority and role of the Bible. He asserts the position of the Bible in a Christian's walk in 2 Timothy 3:16: "All Scripture is breathed out by God and profitable for teaching, for reproof, for correction, and for training in righteousness." Moreover, Christians respond to the Word of God presented in the Bible. John 10:27 says, "My sheep hear my voice, and I know them, and they follow me." The Bible promises to "enlighten your heart" and "make wise the simple."

Birds know about rising thermals that carry them upward without effort; they sense the natural laws tugging at them. A flap of the wing employs chemical reactions, biomechanics, and fluid dynamics to overcome gravity. Birds perhaps know that flapping uses energy, and energy comes from food. Christians consider Jesus and His presentation in the Bible as the "bread of life" that provides deep, spiritual sustenance.

Natural Grace

9

Hiking

Hiking has given me the most consistent contact with nature. I love to walk and talk. The ancient ground and life raging woods settles me and allows thoughts and conversations to flow. When I hike, I am usually well-rested, well-fed, and wearing clean clothes – a great contrast from other outdoor activities. I can hear everything and smell changes in the wind. I sense motion and my feet get to do what they were created to do – settle gracefully on every contorted surface they encounter. You can't really take a walk without your mind and mood being gently altered. A walk lets my mind peacefully process things and lets my dreams rage. It bonds me to friends and family when they are with me. It lets me dream and sense the community of animals when I'm alone.

The ancient ability to walk puts the body in the rhythm for which it was intended. The arms swing, the legs extend, the hip rotates, and the head bobs in a concert of kinesiological choreography. This is a meditative pose, more so than sitting or lying down. The motion pushes noise away and lets you enjoy intimate conversations with God or whoever is walking with you. When there is complete silence, you can hear birds and branches. When hiking, you see how rain collects on the tip of each hemlock needle into a blue-white drop. You see the palette of colors in lichen and moss. You see a whirlwind of leaves being lifted by an eddy of wind. You can try to catch a falling leaf. Henry David Thoreau appreciated the value of pointless walking, claiming, "I have met with but one or two persons in the course of my life who understood the art of Walking, that is, of taking walks – who had the genius, so to speak, for sauntering."

You understand why we must be still and know God.

The forest would be silent if only the best-singing birds would sing. Along with the gentle noises in our area, we hear squeaking tree limbs as they rub in the wind, screaming crows, and chirping chipmunks. We add our own voice to the cacophony, whether gleeful whistling or inner musings. But it is our voice.

While your feet dutifully move you forward, your dreams are made and history recalled. You think of 'what could be' and 'what has been done.' Are you at peace? Are you sucking out all the marrow of life, as Thoreau would ask? Are quiet times filled with the artificial noise of TV, radio, and the internet? Walking will condemn you by its silence and simplicity.

Hikers are not heroes. There is not a lot you can share about a walk in the woods, but it has provided the deepest natural refuge for me. It is what I do when I need to think. If I sit in a chair and pray, I get edgy quickly. My 'to do' list haunts every moment. I need to be away from my home to have time for myself.

In our area, we have many wonderful places to hike, from paths to forest roads. These range from single-width dirt paths to delightfully wide and accessible promenades. There are fewer things more decadent that walking around Canfield Island's pathway while eating donuts and drinking coffee.

When we were toddlers, we figured out how to walk on our two feet. This first sign of liberation from the kingdom of the floor gave us freedom and power. The smile a toddler makes as he gains balance and confidence in this new skill still resides in us. We can go where we want, we can step over obstacles, we can jump and run – any time any place. We bound up steps, or creep down dark hallways.

With each step we take, we can give thanks to the Lord for letting our bodies work. Those who are incapable of walking due to handicap, injury or age are challenged to draw closer to God and thank Him for their disability and the special insights it can provide. They must hold a deeper trust in God and overcome dark thoughts with more spiritual power than most of us. They will enjoy their glorified bodies more richly than most can imagine. Those who can hike know that as we age, this will become more difficult until we can hike no more. We have our time to dance in the wind, and then we must watch others while we wait with faith for the fullness of time, when our faith will be replaced by sight. Then all pain and all evil will be replaced by joy and glory.

Discerning God's will

While we may encounter great moments of peace in nature, we can't rest on this feeling or confuse it with what Colossians 3:15 suggests in stating, "Let the peace of Christ rule in your hearts, to which indeed you were called in one body." This peace is not a sedation produced by warm wind and cool water. It is active. Paul continues to write about the guarding action of Christian peace in Philippians 4:7-9, stating, "The peace of God, which surpasses all understanding, will guard your hearts and minds in Christ Jesus." We are tempted to find direction in emotion as highlighted in the saying, "a person with an experience is never at the mercy of a person with an argument."

If you want to make God laugh, tell Him your plans. So how do we determine the will of God? Let's consider Gideon from Judges 6. Gideon was a brave man chosen by God to save Israel but he had doubts about God's will. He tested God. With fear in his heart, he asked for a sign using dew settling exclusively on or off some fleece he laid out overnight. He used the fleece to determine God's will, but it was an act of doubt, not faith. He wanted physical proof of God's will. This desire for physical signs is still common as we struggle with imperfect faith. We must not confuse a cool wind during a prayer with the real spiritual battle in which we are engaged. We work out our faith in fear and trembling, not with divining natural signs. While I like to think of wonderful events I encounter as a "smile from Jesus", I don't trust in them as providing God's will for me. This is a false worship of signs and nature rather than the almighty Lord.

So are there approaches to discerning God's will? This is an ongoing struggle for me. Discernment can be guided by asking yourself:

1.   Are my actions consistent with God's Word?
2.   Do I have the right gifts for this action?
3.   Is this the right time to take this action?

Lean on others too. Your brothers and sisters in Christ can help you with these inquiries. God will work in them also.

Both our thoughts and actions have to be consistent with God's Word. The Bible's 'arguments' trump our emotions. We must also appreciate both the providential gifts and time we are working in. While God will equip us for His work, we must recognize our special abilities that allow us to serve, while at the same time not cower under what we perceive as weakness that prevents us from serving. We can all be friendly, we can all be brave. Additionally, there are times in our lives when we are prevented from doing certain works. In Acts 16:6, Paul and Silas are specifically "forbidden by the Holy Spirit to speak the word" in certain regions. Amazing! At other times, Paul discerns God's will to serve in places that are not apparent openings, such as in Ephesus where so many adversaries awaited him (1 Corinthians 16:9).

Part II

"The heart has its reasons, which reason does not know."

Blaise Pascal

Natural Grace

10

Creation

Nature can overwhelm us. Nature is fallen and can grip us with fear and submerge us in misery. Addressing these feelings lets us assert the power God gave us over our mind and body. It lets us see how our response to these challenges brings glory to God and makes us more confident and connected with the world around us. However, time spent in our surroundings reveals beauty. It is the embrace of natural beauty that encourages us to immerse ourselves and fully engage the forests, mountains, and waterways in our area.

What is this creation that declares the glory of God? It is more than broad descriptions of plants, mountains, and rivers. It can be described artistically and scientifically, but that will always be incomplete. We can struggle with how it came into existence and why we both love and fear it. We can recognize our inclusion into the natural order and reflect on whether humans are special within the cast of creation.

Let's consider the beauty, science, and philosophy of nature.

11

Beauty of Nature

What makes nature beautiful? What do we find alluring? Nature isn't pure beauty—it is corrupted. You walk on dead vegetation. Almost every animal lives in fear of sudden death.

The Austrian-Swiss poet Rainer Maria Rilke's poems speak of beauty making the inanimate alive, where an ancient torso of Apollo "would burst out of its confines and radiate like a star." Human beauty has its affect: from Helen of Troy's face "launching a thousand ships" seeking to rescue her from Troy to the political intrigue caused by Cleopatra and Antony. The mythological three graces of beauty, charm, and joy entertained the guests of the gods, while the poetry of Sappho and Wordsworth drool with notions of beauty and passion. Beauty can evoke protectiveness. We put beautiful things in museums and ugly things in the garbage. We might kill a cockroach, but not a butterfly. Beauty is a force to be dealt with.

Natural beauty can be connected with the traditional elements of design such as symmetry, repetition, rhythm, balance, proportion, harmony, movement, color, and texture. However, a broader aesthetic assessment can be informed by all the sensory inputs: sight, sound, touch, smell, and taste. The interplays between these senses are complicated.

Interestingly, these aesthetic elements derive from familiarity with our bodies and the world around us. Our breathing gives familiarity to the design concept of repetition. Our heartbeat gives this same familiarity to rhythm, with repeating series of events and occasional variety. The forest is a great example of the rhythm we consider appealing. The forest is comprised of vertical trunks with a variety of lengths and widths. Interspersed is green foliage which is curvilinear, but gradually varies between value and shape within a species and then again between the canopy trees and the understory. We also see rhythm in wood grain and stone, as well as textures that invite us to touch.

Symmetry is appealing. However, things can look artificial if they are perfectly symmetrical, such as a face. Specific face and body proportions are also appealing. The proportional relationship of our hands maintains a constant value of about 1.6 (the 'Golden Ratio') from the extreme digits in our fingers to the metacarpal bones in the palm of our hand. While we can't separate the essence of why we think something is beautiful from our subjective appraisal, we do recognize nature to be beautiful, and we can find joy in that.

* * *

The arts have often portrayed the beauty of nature. For example, the 19th century Hudson River School art movement was a distinctively American approach to sharing the beauty of nature in paintings. These paintings romanticized nature and showed pastoral, idealized compositions of mountainous beauty and dramatic sky. The paintings were initially amalgams of the scenery just north of us, but later, other bucolic settings were included in this movement, all the way out to the Sierra Nevada in California. Jasper Francis Cropsey was one of a number of painters in this tradition who closely connected God with nature. When you see these paintings, you can drink the natural beauty.

Earth Art (or Land Art) is another distinctive American art form where sculptural art is built into the landscape itself. The artwork merges with the land and is not normally protected from eventual disintegration. This art strives to connect with natural features and communicate ideas using the naturally-occurring materials and setting. An example of this art is Robert Smithson's "Spiral Jetty," which is a curved, 1500 foot long jetty that makes a giant spiral in the Great Salt Lake.

Poets have long tapped into natural beauty for inspiration and purpose. A nice example is offered in Joyce Kilmer's "Trees":

> I think that I shall never see
> A poem lovely as a tree.
>
> A tree whose hungry mouth is prest
> Against the earth's sweet flowing breast;
>
> A tree that looks at God all day,
> And lifts her leafy arms to pray;
>
> A tree that may in summer wear
> A nest of robins in her hair;
>
> Upon whose bosom snow has lain;
> Who intimately lives with rain.
>
> Poems are made by fools like me,
> But only God can make a tree.[1]

12

Science of Nature

What is nature made from? It is not comprised of atoms made from a nucleus and orbiting electrons – nature is much more complex. The matter from which nature is comprised is an amalgam of subatomic particles: Higgs bosons, neutrinos, electrons, quarks, photons, and gluons. The behavior of these small particles is described by quantum mechanics, which presents the notion of particles working in fixed bundles (quanta) of energy. For example, light being made from particle-like photons. The relationships between the subatomic particles are described by an inelegant contortion of theories called the Standard Model.

Matter also operates under the weird rules of general relativity, which is not addressed by the Standard Model. General relativity describes the interaction of gravity and space as well as space and time. It addresses the essence of gravity. We know what it does, but struggle to understand what it actually is. While we can accurately use the conveniently understood word "gravity," the gravitational field is actually the same as space. Therefore, space curves and contorts to produce gravity. Additionally, time can be shown to be relative to space/gravity. For example, when a star dies, physicists now propose that it might move beyond a black hole to a hypothetical stage called a "Planck star." Here the matter is completely collapsed into a tiny size that then rebounds outwardly. This collapse and rebound may or may not occur, but what is interesting with this possibility is that it highlights what the extreme compression of space does to time. It essentially stops. The essence of time is different from what we experience in our everyday lives.

As physics delves deeper into nature, we see that energy, matter, and even time are described in probabilistic terms and in connection with interactions rather than their true essence. "Here" and "now" are indexical terms that only make sense in their context. They are not objective statements of what these conditions are, which vary with the observer. The passage of time does not exist as an objective aspect of reality, but as an intuitive grasp of our environment. But is our intuition reliable? Quantum mechanics and general relativity point to the difference between how we sense the world and a more scientifically precise description of it. General relativity presents a very different view than does particle physics and the descriptions offered by quantum mechanics. Where quantum mechanics presents explicit particle-like characteristics of energy and flat space (or at least as a precondition for the required math), general relativity describes curved and continuous space.

We don't see the water molecules in the Susquehanna, but we know we don't want to fall into the river during the spring flooding when the water is cold and rushes against the shores. We are fortunate that great minds can investigate time, space, and the nature of matter. We know that these great minds will gain more insights and richer descriptions of creation. But we also know they won't be able to completely describe creation or matter. Their approaches are based on faith – faith in human reason, which is something we will consider next.

Natural Grace

13

Philosophy of Nature

Those of us who wrestle with faith, reason, and culture may be attracted by the commonly held assertions within the social sciences that knowledge arrives at us through our own interpretation. That is, we process the world around us through our personal lens. Human knowledge is not absolute; it has to be related to the position of the receiver and is influenced by culture and biases.

Philosophy considers the general nature of reality (metaphysics) and the study of knowledge (epistemology). Metaphysics is a broader term for ontology, which seeks to understand the fundamental truth about existence. For Christians, these inquiries are faith based. God is the answer to the metaphysical question, "What is the true or ultimate nature of reality?" Specifically, the Father, Son, and Holy Spirit are in essence (ontologically) equal; however, they exist in a functional (economic) state with distinctive roles and relationships. God's revelation is the answer to the epistemological question, "How do I gain knowledge about the metaphysical?" This revelation is the Bible (special revelation) and nature (general revelation). The Bible also answers the ethical question of moral philosophy — what is right and wrong.

While this may sound like I spent too much time looking at trees, there exists a battle about the undergirding philosophy of science. The philosophies of science establish a foundation for the study of nature. Does science operate in an environment where scientists quickly abandon previous theory in the face of evidence, or is science founded on traditional mental models and group behavior? Two schools of philosophy champion each side. Karl Popper and others argue that science always includes new evidence while Thomas Kuhn and others assert that social forces impede changes to scientific theories.

Some philosophers have extended this inquiry into the limits of scientific method. They argue that the outcomes of revolutionary times in science, such as the acceptance of the Copernican heliocentric model for the solar system, occur when traditional theories are being strongly challenged. During these times, scientists will resist abandoning their traditional theories. Moreover, when science moves beyond its realm of studying the world of nature, it is not doing science but rather abiding the philosophical view of scientism. Scientism asserts we are rationally entitled to only believe what science claims, science is the only (or best) route to truth and meaning.

Data usually drives theories, from 'grounded theory' approaches in the social sciences to inferential statistics. However, data, or in a general sense, evidence, is a product of data acquisition methods. Evidence is also routed through biases connected with how we obtain data and the context under which we acquired it. All of these issues are a threat to objectivity. The interface of evidence and bias can be summarized by the German physicist Werner Heisenberg's (renowned for his 'Heisenberg Uncertainty Principle') assertion that "the world cannot be separated from our perception of it."[1]

Francis Bacon opined about human values and preconceptions intruding into science. He was especially contemptuous of religion's connection with science. In his essay, "The Four Idols", he holds religion in contempt. However, his argument is that "the formation of ideas and axioms by true induction is no doubt the proper remedy for keeping off and clearing idols."[2] What is induction? In Bacon's view, it was gathering and categorizing facts that lead to a truth. Who gets to decide what a fact is? How do you obtain facts about the transcendent, which by definition is beyond the sentient and can't be measured?

Natural science huddles around Darwin's theory of evolution. However, this theory faces problems including the inability to test and verify hypotheses, inability to explain complex biological systems, and semantic debates about natural selection and microevolution. Finally, it is challenged by being unchallengeable. The entrenchment of evolution as dogma ostensibly offers the only scientific gateway into understanding nature. Condescending attitudes are presented to anyone asking question of the orthodoxy. Discussion doesn't seem to be an option. This is a sad state for science. For this reason, it is helpful to consider philosophy, which provides a platform to consider our understanding of nature.

Science is not the only discipline in which foundational principles have to be considered. Philosophy itself has the "principia" of human reason. Therefore, philosophy has to be founded on theology. Why? Because theology has its foundation based on God (principium essendi) and God's revelation (principium cognoscendi). That is the starting point for understanding ultimate truths, and it is founded in faith. A nasty loop when your only god is reason.

We recognize that scientific advances are not always orderly. Some philosophers (e.g. Paul Feyerabend and Stanislav Grof) would consider the whimsy and chaos of individuals as productive and powerful agents of change. Others (e.g., Richard Rorty) considered some final truth to be unattainable or even desirable, which points back to the 18th century Scottish philosopher, David Hume's realization of there being no end point in proving scientific theories. He argued that the contentious and muddy world of scientific (and what Kuhn would call pseudo-science) pursuit is good.

How does this help the Christian ponderer? Approaching knowledge from an interpretive perspective lets us make ticklish forays into science and recognize its limitations. We can join the company of philosophers who recognize that science has a faith in human reason. Human reason has failed us many times from Aristotelian to Newtonian physics, which explains our little world of low speeds and high mass, but fails in universal applications. Ironically, the logical, but faith-based, idea of an eternal universe as described in Fred Hoyle's 1948 "Steady State" theory ironically mocked the "Big Bang" theory. However, ongoing evidence pointed to the Big Bang as the best explanation of creation chronology.

Scripture says that our minds are naturally hostile to God (Romans 8:7) and non-Christians will view theological approaches as foolish (1 Corinthians 2:6-16). Faith in God and the inerrancy of Scripture comes from the Holy Spirit, and Christians can boldly assert this on the first page of their mind's journey. We articulate our "framework" and move on.

Science can give us tools to understand God's creation, and human theories deriving from the scientific method are helpful. But are they always true? No, they are rooted in interpretive understandings that are fine as far as they serve us, but they do not diminish the validity of Scripture. We can operate in two worlds: one of science and helpful theories, and the other as Christians who have faith in the absolute truths offered in Scripture. One of the challenges with using science in broad strokes across society is that it overextends itself. Scientists strive to extrapolate theories beyond what is reproducible. Both cosmology and evolution are examples where science has extended beyond the empirical and into areas that can't be measured or tested. These are interesting conjectures, but not science in the traditional sense of using the scientific method. Interpretive research frameworks, as used in the social sciences, simply recognize that facts and theories are founded on faith in employing human reason and interpretation.

14

God and Nature

Christians think of the metaphysical and transcendent as areas outside the touch of positivistic science. We engage faith in these areas. Therefore, science must be silent – the metaphysical is not the realm of empiricists. This weird, anti-intellectual haze where events can't be measured or tested leaves our enlightened minds troubled. How do we handle the dissonance between science promising to explain everything and the arena of our existence that lies beyond the sentient? We think of Job, where God asks why Job assumes he can ask the questions that are outside Job's purview (Job 38). Or do we think of anti-religious scholars who state axiomatically that theistic descriptions are false? Their declarative statements are shepherded by dense vocabulary and florid language, never asking the question about what areas of valid inquiry exist for science and what areas must it be humbled and silent in response. Can complex biological systems be explained by natural selection? How did the universe start? Saying, "I don't know" should be an option for everyone, including scientists.

Christian faith is a gift from God. Without this faith, we are enslaved to another faith, which is usually our mind and its ostensible ability to be rational. Faith in our mind means we can apply our reasoning in a universal manner.

Studying the marvels of nature is a wonderful thing. Observing nature was entertainment for the ancients. Observing microscope slides and genomic data has provided great insights into the basic composition of life. However, by faith, we see God creating humans as distinctive entities that carry the spark of the divine. From Genesis 1:27, we know, "God created man in his own image, in the image of God he created him; male and female he created them." We know we are loved by God and we were made to be with God for eternity (Jeremiah 31:3, Ecclesiastes 3:11). We further see the closure of the role of Adam in a perfect way: "The first man Adam became a living being; the last Adam became a life-giving spirit" (1 Corinthians 15:45).

God reveals Himself to everyone. Psalm 19:1 states: "The heavens declare the glory of God, and the sky above proclaims his handiwork." Romans 1:18-23 is another passage that describes our rebellion and desire to suppress the truth:

> For the wrath of God is revealed from heaven against all ungodliness and unrighteousness of men, who by their unrighteousness suppress the truth. For what can be known about God is plain to them, because God has shown it to them. For his invisible attributes, namely, his eternal power and divine nature, have been clearly perceived, ever since the creation of the world, in the things that have been made. So they are without excuse. For although they knew God, they did not honor him as God or give thanks to him, but they became futile in their thinking, and their foolish hearts were darkened. Claiming to be wise, they became fools, and exchanged the glory of the immortal God for images resembling mortal man and birds and animals and creeping things.

The relationship between God and nature is recognizing God's ongoing creation, sustenance, and dominion. In Exodus 3:14, God says, "I AM who I AM." God's specific relationship with us is through Jesus Christ, "He is the radiance of the glory of God and the exact imprint of his nature, and he upholds the universe by the word of his power" (Hebrews 1:3).

Natural Grace

15

Final Thoughts

Immersing ourselves in nature can range from watching bird feeder dynamics on a cold winter morning to flying a kite and feeling the wind pull on your hand as you touch the sky. It can be walking waist deep in water while wearing warm waders, or trying to catch a falling leaf in autumn. You learn silly things, like how goldfinches are chased away from the birdfeeder by nuthatches but not chickadees, or that a falling leaf is very difficult to catch (try it!)

We revel in nature's beauty. We find hidden depths of personal ability as we contend with the challenges nature presents. Our response to nature can't be captured, relived, saved, or frozen in any way. They are living experiences; their joy is connected with their transitory nature. They are ephemeral and beautiful, like a bird on the upstroke of its flapping wing. We are promised more beautiful times in the future. Beauty so profound that the description of restoration in the book of Revelation only presents paradise in ways we can vaguely understand.

Until then, we wait in faith, enjoying what God has blessed us with in our beautiful part of the world. We reflect on the transcendent as we walk in an environment of sensory overload. Pollen pushed by refreshing breezes, cacophonous tree frogs, and chilling snow let us enjoy the deeper truths around us. These truths manifest themselves in peace of mind and artistry. Gordon MacDonald offers the following insight:

> The best kind of thinking is accomplished when it is done in the context of reverence for God's kingly reign over all creation. It is sad to see great thinking and artistic work accomplished by men and women who have no interest in uncovering knowledge of the Creator.[1]

Pursuing pleasure is our common vice. We seek to escape struggles by watching TV, surfing the internet, and playing video games. Engaging nature is also a pursuit of pleasure, but it is quiet and leaves you alone with your thoughts. Nature does not infuse you with someone else's creation— it presents God's creation. You don't swim in electronic marvels that scream at you and don't give you time to blink or think. However, we are all humbled when we compare the time spent pursuing fun versus the time spent in prayer or Bible study.

Christianity is not a hip, antiestablishment lifestyle. It is worn like a nice suit and polished shoes. You don't get admiring stares or special recognition. You are just, 'one of them.' You are in the same group as everyone else, from musicians wearing crosses and singing about sex, to ministers who take advantage of their privilege. You are among the hypocrites who confuse children and can cause darkness in souls. Who wants to be in that group? However, Christianity is not a costume we put on or take off. Christians are known by how they respond to the Holy Spirit. "The fruit of the Spirit is: love, joy, peace, patience, kindness, goodness, faithfulness, gentleness, and self-control" (Galatians 5:22). This fruit of the Spirit is deep character changes that come from God's grace. They do not produce salvation – they reflect God's love into the world around you. If you measure your faith by looking at others, you will never be satisfied. "How can he claim to be a Christian and still do that?" is a constant refrain we make. However, we are all sinners in thought, word, and deed, so we live hypocritical lives. However, those who are born again (regenerated) ask for forgiveness and seek to be obedient to God's will. They don't say, 'everyone else is doing it' and continue to live in sin. They repent and live lives that God intended them to live. As it says in 1 John 1:9: "If we confess our sins, he is faithful and just to forgive us our sins and to cleanse us from all unrighteousness."

There is no step-by-step instruction for managing our life. While the wisdom literature in Scripture, especially Proverbs, can be very practical, Philippians 4:8-9 guides us on how our minds should process the world around us:

> Whatever is true, whatever is honorable, whatever is just, whatever is pure, whatever is lovely, whatever is commendable, if there is any excellence, if there is anything worthy of praise, think about these things.

In nature, we don't have to fear what other people think. We don't have to posture. We can be fully ourselves, and the results of our actions are rapid and sure. Our insecurities are obvious when outdoors. We lay awake at night listening to unfamiliar noises, or worry about getting hurt far away from help.

Our fear and insecurity when dealing with other people can shackle us to a stake of hypocrisy. We act differently than we believe. We cast deeply-held values aside for the sake of social conformity. Proverbs 29:25

reflects this problem: "The fear of man brings a snare: but those who put trust in the Lord shall be safe."

The confidence born by doing challenging things can help liberate us from this insecurity. However, developing expertise in a skill is no promise of self-esteem. That is a false promise. We recognize our skills and abilities are gifts of God, from our physical abilities to our intellect itself.

The only enduring security is placing our trust in something that does not change and loves us unconditionally. This desire for a rock-solid foundation is what drives our spiritual quest. Many people seek this foundation and follow enticing paths that satisfy both their spiritual thirst and social needs. Others reject the search and find solace in alcohol, drugs, or an ongoing pursuit of pleasure. Some find a foundation in religion. Religion-light is a wonderful opiate, giving a temporary, emotional refuge, like watching a good movie. However, the only true security and confidence is found in Jesus Christ and the Word that He gave us in the Bible.

We take up this love relationship imperfectly. We don't hold up our end of the relationship. But we are forgiven and never released from the hug of pure love and eternal grace. This is why the book of Psalms ends with, "let everything that has breath praise the Lord!" (Psalm 150:6).

Natural Grace

Appendix

Safety

I don't like writing about the natural beauty in our area and then dragging out every horror story I can think of to impress or scare. Your house and car are much more dangerous than anything you will encounter outside. However, moving from the world of indoor safety to the unknowns of nature satiates a need for exploration and wonder. It is a humble attempt to master our universe – to resist intimidation by all the things out there that want to seemingly hurt you.

I didn't really want to write this section, but then my 'grown up' gene kicked in. I thought since this writing is an introduction to some outdoor activities it would be wise to include some comments about safety in the same work. However, there are many books, videos, and other sources of information from people much wiser than me to which you should refer.

Backpacking and hiking

There is a lot of discussion about what equipment is required for backpacking. Light is good, but it is all a matter of compromises. One of the saddest encounters I can recall backpacking was when I found a single, new water shoe on the West Rim Trail. Later on the trail, I encountered another backpacker who asked if I had seen someone struggling on the trail. I said I had not, but reported the single water shoe I found. There are no stream crossings on the West Rim Trail. In putting this all together, I think a new backpacker loaded up a ton of gear and headed out. I can only imagine his misery. I have seen people, including myself, who don't have the latest ultralight gear. We have used giant tents, rectangular sleeping bags, and ancient packs. That doesn't matter as long as you get out there.

The three hardest things about backpacking are: 1) getting to the trailhead, 2) going up hills, and 3) sleeping. I deal with these as follows. First, trailhead locating and car parking challenges compel me to go to familiar haunts. Second, going up inclines with a full pack requires me to shut down my mind and let my feet do the thinking. Finally, I don't sleep well the first night and I accept that fate.

In terms of health and safety, water purification is probably the most important issue. Even clean-looking, fast-flowing water can be contaminated. For water purification, I use a water microfilter rather than UV or purification pills. The filter works well because I rarely travel in valleys along creeks and rivers. Instead, I need to tap into the tiny streams that ooze out of the mountain rocks. This water often collects in slowly-draining pools and isn't as sediment free as flowing water. It is easier to pump out the water than to try to scoop it out with a water bottle. I also take a few purification pills as an emergency backup to the filter.

I usually take one liter in a water bottle and 2 liters in a plastic soda bottle. The Institute of Medicine recommends 3 liters of water consumption per day for men and 2.2 liters per day for women. However, food provides roughly twenty percent of your required water. Dark urine means you are dehydrated.

Weakness, nausea, headache, lightheadedness, and muscle cramps are signs of heat exhaustion. If you have these symptoms, rehydrate with water and a sports drink if you have it. Move into the shade and rest. If heat exhaustion isn't treated, it can turn into heat stroke as the body temperature rises to dangerous levels. Some of the identifiers of heat stroke are disorientation and dry skin with lack of sweating. This dangerous condition requires immediate cooling with water and hospital transport.

The most common problem you will encounter is bugs. When gnats or mosquitoes are really bad, I use a mosquito head net and insect repellent. I think I have only gotten ticks in my yard.

Ticks can be removed by putting a lubricant on a gauze pad or wadded paper towel and rubbing around the tick close to its head. I use either petroleum jelly or liquid soap. It always works. There are other ways to remove ticks, but I like this technique the best.

Unfortunately, ticks transmit Lyme disease and this illness is another sad reminder of the corruption of nature due to our fall in Eden. Half the time the disease will present a red "bull's-eye" rash called 'erythema migrans'. Otherwise, it might just present "flu-like symptoms", which makes it hard to identify.

The Mayo Clinic offers the following advice for recognizing Lyme disease:

Early signs and symptoms:
A small, red bump often appears at the site of a tick bite or tick removal and resolves over a few days. This is normal after a tick bite and does not indicate Lyme disease.
However, these signs and symptoms may occur within a month after you've been infected:
- Rash. From 3 to 30 days after an infected tick

bite, an expanding red area might appear that sometimes clears in the center, forming a bull's-eye pattern. The rash (erythema migrans) expands slowly over days and can spread to 12 inches (30 centimeters) across. It is typically not itchy or painful. Erythema migrans is one of the hallmarks of Lyme disease. Some people develop this rash at more than one place on their bodies.

- Flu-like symptoms. Fever, chills, fatigue, body aches and a headache may accompany the rash.

Later signs and symptoms:

If untreated, new signs and symptoms of Lyme infection might appear in the following weeks to months. These include:

- Erythema migrans appearing in other areas of your body.
- Joint pain. Bouts of severe joint pain and swelling are especially likely to affect your knees, but the pain can shift from one joint to another.
- Neurological problems. Weeks, months or even years after infection, you might develop inflammation of the membranes surrounding your brain (meningitis), temporary paralysis of one side of your face (Bell's palsy), numbness or weakness in your limbs, and impaired muscle movement.

Signs and symptoms caused by the bacterium Borrelia mayonii may also include:

- Nausea and vomiting
- Diffuse rashes (rather than a single bull's-eye rash commonly associated with Lyme disease)

Less common signs and symptoms:

Several weeks after infection, some people develop:

- Heart problems, such as an irregular heartbeat. Heart problems rarely last more than a few days or weeks.
- Eye inflammation.
- Liver inflammation (hepatitis).
- Severe fatigue.

Source: Mayo Clinic,

http://www.mayoclinic.org/diseases-conditions/lyme-disease/basics/symptoms/con-20019701.

Plants can be a problem too. The pain from the stinging nettle plant goes away magically within about five minutes. I usually encounter these around streams. Don't scratch the area and try to wash it off with water right away. Other topical treatments such as soap, aloe vera, and hydrocortisone can also be used. Tape can be used to draw out the tiny needles but I have never needed to do this.

You may encounter poison ivy, but probably won't see poison sumac or oak in our area. "Leaflets three, leave it be" is the old mnemonic for recalling the look of these plants. However, most plants look like they have "leaflets three," so that advice doesn't seem to help. The leaves will carry a red hue that starts showing in the summer. They are usually shiny, but not always.

The problem with plants is you can't investigate plant taxonomy when you are trying to make time. Wear shoes and socks, and you are in pretty good shape for walking. Poison ivy can grow as a vine, so you can be exposed elsewhere. Recently, I walked into large group of poison ivy while wearing sandals. It was kind of funny in a weird way. I stopped and looked around and thought, "I shouldn't be here." I gingerly made my way out the mass of nasty stuff and waded into a nearby lake. If you think you are exposed, wash off the area with soap and water as quickly as possible. Unlike stinging nettles, poison ivy exposure leads to a worsening rash for most people. Additionally, the urushiol oil from poison ivy will linger on clothes and can spread. Don't burn poison ivy because the smoke becomes a carrier of the oil and can be inhaled, which is dangerous. I have had only one bad exposure to poison ivy that needed medical treatment. Once I sense itchiness, I quickly wash the area and I am okay.

If a rash develops, don't scratch it. Take an antihistamine (e.g. Benadryl) and apply a topical ointment such as hydrocortisone or calamine lotions. You need immediate medical treatment if you have an allergic reaction as might be indicated by shortness of breath, trouble swallowing, or swelling around the rash.

Unfortunately, we have venomous rattlesnakes and copperheads in our area. Yes, they are good for the ecosystem, but so are mosquitoes and I don't like them either. I have never been bitten by these snakes but have encountered them. My approach is not to worry about them, because as with ticks and nasty plants, you will just go crazy and stay at home watching movies and playing video games.

First aid recommendations for snakebites have changed over the years. The recommended procedure from the Mayo Clinic is:

- Remain calm and move beyond the snake's striking distance.
- Remove jewelry and tight clothing before you start to swell.
- Position yourself, if possible, so that the bite is at or below the level of your heart.
- Clean the wound, but don't flush it with water. Cover it with a clean, dry dressing.
- Don't use a tourniquet or apply ice.

- Don't cut the wound or attempt to remove the venom.
- Don't drink caffeine or alcohol, which could speed the rate at which your body absorbs venom.
- Don't try to capture the snake. Try to remember its color and shape so that you can describe it, which will help in your treatment.

Source: Mayo Clinic, http://www.mayoclinic.org/first-aid/first-aid-snake-bites/basics/art-20056681.

We do have black bears in our area, but they are shy and shouldn't be a safety problem. They do want your food though! This is what the National Park Service recommends if you encounter a bear:

- Identify yourself by talking calmly so the bear knows you are a human and not a prey animal. Remain still; stand your ground but slowly wave your arms. Help the bear recognize you as a human. It may come closer or stand on its hind legs to get a better look or smell. A standing bear is usually curious, not threatening.
- Stay calm and remember that most bears do not want to attack you; they usually just want to be left alone. Bears may bluff their way out of an encounter by charging and then turning away at the last second. Bears may also react defensively by woofing, yawning, salivating, growling,

snapping their jaws, and laying their ears back. Continue to talk to the bear in low tones; this will help you stay calmer, and it won't be threatening to the bear. A scream or sudden movement may trigger an attack. Never imitate bear sounds or make a high-pitched squeal.

- Pick up small children immediately.
- Hike and travel in groups. Groups of people are usually noisier and smellier than a single person. Therefore, bears often become aware of groups of people at greater distances, and because of their cumulative size, groups are also intimidating to bears.
- Make yourselves look as large as possible (for example, move to higher ground).
- Do NOT allow the bear access to your food. Getting your food will only encourage the bear and make the problem worse for others.
- Do NOT drop your pack as it can provide protection for your back and prevent a bear from accessing your food.
- If the bear is stationary, move away slowly and sideways; this allows you to keep an eye on the bear and avoid tripping. Moving sideways is also non-threatening to bears. Do NOT run, but if the bear follows, stop and hold your ground. Bears can run as fast as a racehorse both uphill and

down. Like dogs, they will chase fleeing animals. Do NOT climb a tree. Both grizzlies and black bears can climb trees.

- Leave the area or take a detour. If this is impossible, wait until the bear moves away. Always leave the bear an escape route.

- Be especially cautious if you see a female with cubs; never place yourself between a mother and her cub, and never attempt to approach them. The chances of an attack escalate greatly if she perceives you as a danger to her cubs.

Bear Attacks

Bear attacks are rare; most bears are only interested in protecting food, cubs, or their space. However, being mentally prepared can help you have the most effective reaction. Every situation is different, but below are guidelines on how brown bear attacks can differ from black bear attacks. Help protect others by reporting all bear incidents to a park ranger immediately. Above all, keep your distance from bears!

Brown/Grizzly Bears:

If you are attacked by a brown/grizzly bear, leave your pack on and PLAY DEAD. Lay flat on your stomach with your hands clasped behind your neck. Spread your legs to make it harder for the bear to turn you over. Remain still until the bear leaves the area. Fighting back usually increases the intensity of such attacks. However, if the attack persists, fight back vigorously. Use whatever you have at hand to hit the bear in the face.

Black Bears:

If you are attacked by a black bear, DO NOT PLAY DEAD. Try to escape to a secure place such as a car or building. If escape is not possible, try to fight back using any object available. Concentrate your kicks and blows on the bear's face and muzzle.
Source: National Park Service,
https://www.nps.gov/subjects/bears/safety.htm.

Other safety issues are more common sense. Watch where you sleep. Don't sleep under dead limbs or trees, and watch the weather when in flash flood areas (this concern is especially true for caves). Tie your food bag to a rope and elevate it overhead to reduce bear scavenging. The experts say you should elevate the food 12 feet high and 6 feet from the trunk. You are supposed to sleep 100 feet away from where you eat.

Heat from a campfire can cause snow to dump from overhead branches, and smooth rocks can hold water that can explode when heated (which is really scary!).

There is a lot of information available on setting up camps that I don't want to repeat here except to note that a good night's sleep is very important, so prepare the area under your tent and/or sleeping bag as best you can by cleaning up debris and avoiding damp or unlevel ground. In extreme weather such as cold and rain, you need to keep some set of clothing dry for sleeping. It is okay to get wet when it is warm, but it is no fun sleeping in wet clothes. When it is cold, the situation is more dangerous.

You need liquid fuel (like white gas) for operating a stove in very cold weather. Butane doesn't vaporize at low temperatures (below 31 degrees F) and isobutane has problems when it gets very cold (below 11 degrees F). You can heat up the gas canister fuel, or keep it in a pan of liquid water to keep it above freezing. Flames of any sort (including candles) can produce carbon monoxide that can be deadly in an enclosed tent. Carbon monoxide is invisible and odorless, so you can't detect its presence. Therefore, don't sleep with a flame on.

Finally, as with many outdoor excursions, leave word about what you are up to with someone you trust. You should give them your location and when you expect to return. I add 24-36 hours to my expected return time for short backpacking trips. Don't just say the date and time – write it on a piece of paper. If you haven't called in by that time, they should call the police and ask for search and rescue help.

Climbing

I have not been seriously injured rock climbing, but it can be dangerous. I am also too easily frightened to take on any crazy climbs. I have had to 'retire' a couple of cliffs because the rocks were too crumbly and loose. Only once have I been hit by a falling rock (and it was the back of my hand), but it was an invigorating reminder of the fragility of our sedimentary stone. The standard warning on climbing gear is:

> Climbing is an inherently dangerous activity that may result in serious injury or death. It is the sole responsibility of the purchaser or user of any climbing equipment to get proper instruction and to act safely and with caution while using this equipment.

There are five types of climbing in our region: top roping, traditional ('trad'), sport climbing, bouldering, and ice climbing. In top roping, you secure an anchor at the top of the cliff, in traditional climbing you set up anchors as you go, and sport climbing uses pre-established anchors. Bouldering is climbing small cliffs or boulders without ropes. You have a crash pad underneath you and friends who spot you. Falls are short drops to the crash pad rather than rope braked descents. Ice climbing uses a lot of equipment. It involves using crampons and ice axes to make your way up a frozen waterfall. It is like traditional climbing, except the anchors are different.

Rappelling is a lot of fun too. Rappelling is a controlled slide down a rope from a top anchor. You can rappel off cliffs that you couldn't normally climb and it is a great way to get into your own vertical world. This is normally how you start top roping as you set up the anchor on top of the cliff and rappel down two lines to the bottom. Indoor climbing gyms let you work out techniques and spend more time actually climbing than traveling to the cliffs, setting up and dealing with bugs.

Because I wrote about rock climbing, I thought I would offer the following guidelines. However, you really need proper training before climbing.

Rock climbing doesn't require a lot of gear and doesn't have to be hard or crazy. This isn't meant as a rock climbing manual, but all you need to get started is a rope, harness, nylon webbing, three locking carabineers (one large carabineer is helpful), a belay device, and a helmet. Unlike a lot of outdoor activities, you can't take shortcuts with rock climbing equipment. You also need to know how to tie figure-eight and water knots. Rock climbing shoes squeeze your feed so you can use the edges better. They also have soft rubber bottoms that help you stick to the rock. Powdered chalk let's your hands grip better. You can make a harness with rope but commercial harnesses are much more comfortable.

For top roping and rappelling, attach two runs of nylon tubular webbing to two different trees. You can make a loop with the webbing by tying the ends together with a water knot. You can also make sliding loops with a figure-eight knot. Attach the carabineers to each webbing loop; this gives you two separate anchors. It is acceptable to use one anchor if you really trust it. The tree needs to be healthy, well-rooted, and at least 6 inches in diameter. Anchors can also be set up in rock cracks with a variety of devices such as nuts and cams.

Run your climbing rope through the carabineers and throw both ends over the cliff, making sure they reach the bottom. From the bottom of the cliff, attach your belay device (I usually use an ATC or 'air traffic controller') to the rope and your harness with a locking carabineer. Put on your helmet and test the setup by leaning back.

If you are top roping, your belayer also wears a harness and attaches the ATC to their harness. The climber runs a loop through their harness that is tied up in a figure eight-knot. The belay can also be attached to another anchor, such as a tree, instead of the belayer.

This is necessary if there is a big weight difference between the climber and belayer.

For rappelling, you can run both ropes through your ATC (or other device). Alternatively, you can tie one end of the rope to the anchor and rappel using one run of rope. I usually rappel down a cliff first and then top rope up. Therefore, I need to rappel down a doubled rope. I usually make a loop of small diameter rope (cordelette) and attach it from my leg strap to the rope with a prusik knot so it will brake for me in case my hand slips or I am knocked out. None of this has ever happened, but it is good to be super safe when you can.

It is good to tie a figure-eight knot at each end of each rope so you don't accidentally rappel off the end of the rope. You may wonder if you can use a bowline instead of a figure-eight for making a loop. They are both strong knots that can be easily untied. I use figure-eight knots for climbing and bowlines for sailing. I don't ask why – I just do what is traditional. I do like a figure-eight because it is easy to tie and easy to visually determine that it is correctly tied.

Practice all these techniques on a tree, on a beam in your basement, or wherever you are most comfortable learning the knots and techniques. Before climbing or rappelling, lean back while on level ground to test that the anchor holds, your knots are good, your carabineers are locked, and your belay system works smoothly. Don't go if you are not confident in your belay or anchor system. There are auto locking belay devices available; I use the ATC because I can use it for both belaying and rappelling. However, the auto locking devices are safer.

Dynamic, 10.5 mm rope is a nice reliable size. I use a lighter 9.8 mm dynamic rope if I am carrying it far. I also have an 11 mm static line for just rappelling. Dynamic rope acts like a shock-absorbing bungee cord and must be used when traditional or sport climbing, where you could fall some distance before the anchor catches you – twice the distance from you to your last anchor. Top roping and rappelling can use the non-elastic static line because you don't need the shock-absorbing properties of dynamic rope. However, you can use dynamic rope for these as well.

Ropes should be retired after five years, when there is outer sheath damage, or after several big falls. Check the manufacturer information for specifics. I use 1 inch tubular nylon for wrapping around a tree for an anchor, but there are other advanced materials such as Dynex that are much thinner. You can also make a perfectly safe harness by using rope or webbing alone. You need 6 feet of it, and you tie it around your waist and between your legs. It is not that comfortable, but it is very safe and much improved over the "swami" waist belt that I used many years ago. The helmet is needed

Natural Grace

in case you fall and smash against the rock, but the most important use in our area is to protect your head from falling rocks. This is a potential problem with some of the crumbling cliffs in our area.

Over the years, I have gotten other gear for traditional climbing. These include different type of anchors that can be jammed into a crack in the rocks, or more beautifully elaborate anchors that have cams that expand and lock into cracks. I have also had a lot of fun with ascenders, which let you shimmy up the rope. You can make these from prusik knots, but they are cumbersome to slide up the rope.

Caving

Some friends and I were exploring a wild cave in Indiana and after several hours, we happened to notice stars above us. This was a confusing sight for someone with dirty glasses and vision focused on what laid only immediately ahead. We stopped to gather our wits and we figured out we were looking at the night sky (we had started in daylight). As it turns out, the cave we were exploring intersected a limestone quarry and we were about to walk off the ledge and into the quarry. Fortunately, we stopped just in time and turned around!

Caves are the most delicate ecosystem in our area. Very few people travel in caves, and spelunkers can do tremendous damage such as spreading fungal

138

disease and breaking formations. The distinctive dangers associated with caves are getting stuck and lost.

Experts recommend a headlamp and two additional sources of light. I used to duct tape two flashlights to my hard hat, which worked very well. You do a lot of crawling, so I ironed patches on the knees of my insulated coveralls. I guess kneepads are better, but I have never used them. Caves maintain a cool temperature, usually in the low 50s, so dress for a cool, spring day. Most of the caves I have explored in Indiana are wet and muddy – a kid's dream. However, this environment makes for a cold, wet adult.

Know the weather if you are going into a wet cave. Watch your step and the flooring below you, it can drop into deep seams or shafts. Don't cave alone. It is also very important to tell someone you trust your location and expected return time. Add whatever time buffer you think is appropriate. After that time, instruct them to call the police for search and rescue help.

Fundamentally, you need to remember you have to get out of whatever you got into, and no one can reach you quickly if you are injured.

Boating

Our desire to go out on the water can be dangerous with hypothermia and drowning as the principle dangers. Boating in the spring puts you on top of surprisingly cold water and you need to be especially careful. Running the creeks adds the additional concern of head injury.

Strange things can happen on boats. Boats tip over and people tip over. People get hit by sail booms, dislocate shoulders, have legs fall asleep, get stuck, etc. A sunny, peaceful day can take on a mean and dangerous character on the water. The equipment required on boats can really save your life.

Detailed boating regulations are available online, but the minimum requirements for state waters are:

- One personal floatation device (PFD) for each person on board. One throwable device if the boat is over 16 ft. Adults must wear a PFD on kayaks, canoes, and boats under 16 feet from November through April.
- A sound producing device such as a whistle.
- One Coast Guard approved B1 marine fire extinguisher for motor boats.
- Night signals when operating at night.

Most everyone should have something with which to bail water. Kayakers in creeks should wear helmets, and sailors should have an emergency paddle. Again, specific regulations should be found online.

Big boats have a lot of inertia. They move slowly, but with great authority. Watch where you put your body parts when docking – let the boat take any impact, not you. Boats can leak rapidly via failed through-hulls, including propeller shafts. You always need a backup plan for rapid flooding, such as plugs, bilge pumps, and bailers (e.g. a bucket).

The basic knots needed are a bowline for mooring lines and sail halyards and a square knot or sheet bend (which I prefer) for tying ropes together. Finally, you often need to know how to belay a cleat. This is where you twist a line around a cleat. The old Navy yarn is: one wrap to hold a man, two to hold a horse, and three to hold the devil himself.

The United States Coast Guard Auxiliary (USCG Aux) and the United States Power Squadrons (USPS) provide excellent training programs on boat safety and operation. Please take one of their courses.

Armor of God

We don't take a hike wearing business clothes. We need to think about how we should dress for the day in terms of the spiritual struggle in which we are engaged. We have to strive to put on the armor of God, which is Christ. Then God's truth becomes our truth and we are truthful. We learn truth through Scripture and preaching, and we prepare ourselves for days of war during our days of peace.

Because the ultimate challenges are spiritual, I leave you with this classic verse describing God's protection.

> Finally, be strong in the Lord and in the strength of his might. Put on the whole armor of God, that you may be able to stand against the schemes of the devil. For we do not wrestle against flesh and blood, but against the rulers, against the authorities, against the cosmic powers over this present darkness, against the spiritual forces of evil in the heavenly places. Therefore take up the whole armor of God, that you may be able to withstand in the evil day, and having done all, to stand firm. Stand therefore, having fastened on the belt of truth, and having put on the breastplate of righteousness, and, as shoes for your feet, having put on the readiness given by the gospel of peace. In all circumstances take up the shield of faith, with which you can extinguish all the flaming darts of the evil one; and take the helmet of salvation, and the sword of the Spirit, which is the word of God, praying at all times in the Spirit, with all prayer and supplication. (Ephesians 6:10-18)

Natural Grace

Notes

Forward

1. Many religions believe that God is present in plants and animals. However, even these animistic adherents use damaging techniques such as fishing by water poisoning and hunting by large scale forest burns. These techniques are used even when these actions present some conflict with belief systems. [Kalland, Arne 2001, 'Indigenous knowledge: prospects and limitation', in Ellen, R., Parkes, P. & Bicker, A. (Eds.) *Indigenous environmental knowledge and its transformation: Critical anthropological perspectives*. Reading, UK: Harwood Academic Publishers, 2001, 319-331.]

Chapter 1   Introduction

1. Seuss, Dr. *Oh, The Places You'll Go!* New York: Random House, 1990.

2. I have a lot of stories about my kids in here but the story telling sharpened my senses, so please excuse the indulgence. I don't have patience for obtuse, long-winded poetry, even though I write obtuse, long-winded poems. Below is an extract from one of my poems that I am burying back here because who reads the "Notes"

section (or poetry for that matter)? This approach risks presenting you with something you might experience when selecting a greeting card, but I hope you like it because it describes the power of fatherhood on me. *I never thought that my ascent would be/To reach down and hold a small hand/Warrior man died in this dream/And "daddy" is my only scream.*

Chapter 4   Boating
1. Vos, Johannes G. *The Westminster Larger Catechism, a Commentary*, G. I Williamson (Ed.) Phillipsburg, NJ: Presbyterian and Reformed Publishing, 2002, 181-185, 317. This reference presents a good discussion of backsliding and assurance of salvation.
2. Talbot, Mark. *The Signs of True Conversion.* Wheaton, IL: Crossway Books, 2000, 20. These are the author's words, but I structured them differently than the original.
3. Luther, Martin. *Concerning Christian Liberty.* Vol. XXXVI, Part 6. The Harvard Classics. New York: P.F. Collier & Son, 1909–14; Bartleby.com, 2001. www.bartleby.com/36/6/.

Chapter 5   Downhill Skiing
1. Spurgeon, Charles. *The Power in Prayer.* New Kensington, PA: Whitaker House, 1996, 151.

Chapter 7   Caving
1. Dante Alighieri, *The Divine Comedy, Hell, Canto XXXIV*, Ann Arbor: Borders Classics, 2004, 258.
2. Lovecraft, H.P., "Lurking Fear." In *HP Lovecraft The Complete Fiction.* New York: Barnes and Noble, 2011, 234.

Chapter 11 Beauty of Nature
1. Kilmer, Joyce. *Trees and Other Poems*. New York: Doubleday Doran and Co., 1914, 18. https://en.wikipedia.org/wiki/Trees_(poem)#Citations.

Chapter 13 Philosophy of Nature
1. Hilgevoord, Jan and Uffink, Jos. "The Uncertainty Principle." In *The Stanford Encyclopedia of Philosophy*, Spring 2014 Edition, Edward N. Zalta (Ed.), 2014. https://plato.stanford.edu/archives/spr2014/entries/qt-uncertainty.
2. Bacon, Francis, "The Four Idols" In *The World of Ideas, 6th Edition,* Lee Jacobus (Ed.) Boston: Bedford/St. Martin's, 2002), 420.

Chapter 15 Final Thoughts
1. MacDonald, Gordon. *Ordering Your Private World.* Nashville: Thomas Nelson, 2003, 113.

Appendix
The sources for Lyme disease identification, snakebite treatment and bear safety described in the appendix are shown in the text to clarify that these were authoritative sources and not my musings. These referenced sources were the Mayo Clinic and the National Park Service. While I'm a licensed EMT, I stand on much taller shoulders regarding medical treatment.

The biggest dangers are "the schemes of the devil," and the only protection from those is in Christ; therefore, the armor of God verse from Ephesians 6 is the most important part of this appendix and it comes from the greatest source.

Natural Grace

Suggested Reading

When I was in college and trying to harmonize my faith and reason, I read a book that promised to help with this pursuit. It was so poorly done that it inflamed my doubts as it made giant, illogical leaps.

Being a Christian doesn't mean turning off your mind or being opposed to science. You need to connect your faith with your reasoning abilities. After all, we are logical beings. A study Bible can be very helpful when you read Scripture because it offers helpful commentary for most verses.

A suggested reading section could be incredibly long but I appreciate you reading to this point – so many things compete for your time. Below are a handful of books that may be helpful. In the end, the Bible is your best source for God's truth; however, the authors below can help you resolve questions. Except for *Mere Christianity*, these books are topical references. You can look up specific areas of interest and read about them, you don't have to plow through them cover to cover. Your pastor is the principal non-Biblical source for presenting and clarifying God's Word. If you don't belong to a church, join one.

Copan, Paul. *How Do You Know You're Not Wrong?* Grand Rapids, MI: BakerBooks, 2005.

Keller, Timothy, *The Reason for God: Belief in an Age of Skepticism.* New York: Riverhead Books, 2008.

Lewis, CS. *Mere Christianity.* New York: MacMillan, 1952.

Poythress, Vern, *Redeeming Science: A God-Centered Approach.* Wheaton, IL: Crossway Books, 2006.

Sproul, RC. *Essential Truths of the Christian Faith.* Carol Stream, IL: Tyndale House Publishers, 1992.

Acknowledgements

I wish to thank the Rev. Dr. Wayne Brauning, a good friend and a retired pastor who reviewed this writing to assure that I did not dishonor Christ in this work. I appreciate the powerful intellect and encouragement he shared with me.

Thanks also go to Rick Taylor, an old friend who knows me better than most. He has a heart for Christ and deep desire to serve His kingdom. I appreciate Rick's care and compassion in assuring this writing was a faithful witness and logically constructed.

God blessed me with my wife Beth. Not only did she review this work but was always eager and available to talk about this project. Love seems like a too common word to express our relationship and I thank her for her ongoing support of my disparate endeavors. God also blessed me with my children, Eric and Elayna. They were gracious in letting me share some of our stories and expressed great love and patience with me as their father. It has been a privilege to be their dad. Elayna was also the proofreader for this work. She did a thorough job and provided many valuable comments.